SACRED ELEPHANT

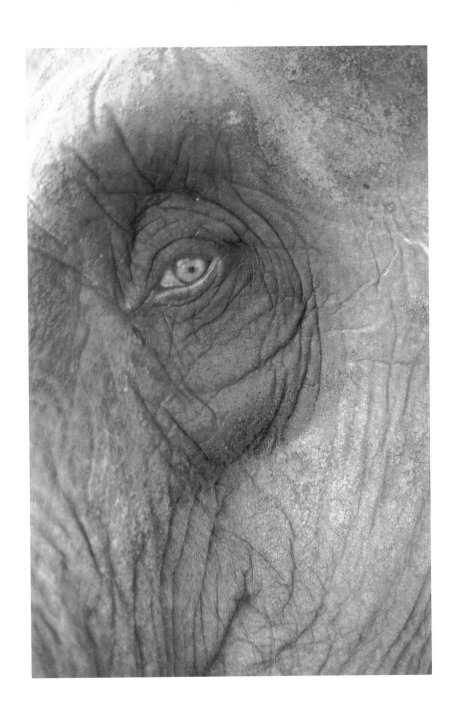

SACRED ELEPHANT

Heathcote Williams

HARMONY BOOKS/NEW YORK

Nature's great masterpiece, an Elephant . . .

John Donne, *Progress of the Soul* XXXIX

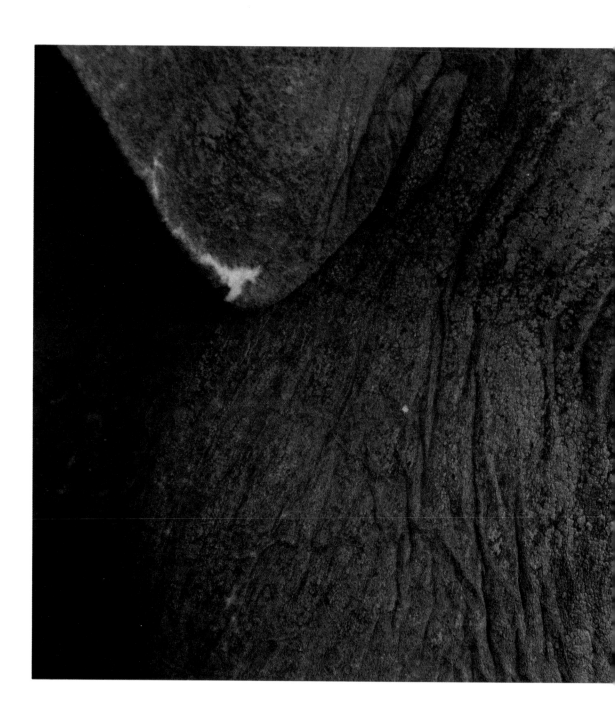

Contents

Behold now behemoth, which I made with thee . . .
chief of the ways of God.

Job 40

The shape of an African elephant's ear
Is the shape of Africa.

The shape of an Indian elephant's ear
Is the shape of India . . .

As if Nature had kept an ear to the ground
When listening to the elephant's territorial requests.
There are few such striking simulacra
Giving human beings a poetic licence to the landscape –
Save perhaps Italy, ˙
Shaped like a wizened jack-boot.

Brahma concealed in each of the animals a profound secret:
The secret of the mystic syllables, *amsvara*,
He concealed in the horse;
The secret of internality
In the cow;
The secret of prophecy in the chameleon;
The secret of longevity in the crow.

In the elephant
'. . . a beast of the moon with crescent tusks
Who has emerged from the churning of the seas . . .'

He said he had concealed wisdom.

The elephant now has a depleted population the size of Willesden
And we are not wise.

It hasn't been for want of good public relations:
Alexander the Great chose the elephant as a symbol of might;

Minerva, the Goddess of Wisdom,
Had the head of an elephant towering above her own,
And elephants pulling her chariots of Knowledge;
To the early Christians the elephant was the Bearer of All
    Infirmities,
And Lord Protector, treading serpents underfoot.
In China, the elephant, *Da Hsiang*, was a beast with power
    over Nature:
The Tantric monk Pu K'ung, in the eighth century,
Joined in meditation with elephants to shift clouds,
Commenting, 'It is easy with such allies to procure rain or
    sunshine,
Though still difficult to rid the country of evil-doers.'
The Romans believed the elephant was a religious animal:
Pliny observed it 'worshipping the sun and stars,
And purifying itself at the new moon,
Bathing in the river, and invoking the heavens.'
The Romans have departed,
But the elephant still stands in introspective silence
At sunrise

And at sunset,
As if in prayer.

In Hinduism, the elephant mounts a tortoise
To support a vessel which holds a lotus:
An indication of the Heath Robinson route we may all take to
    ecstasy;

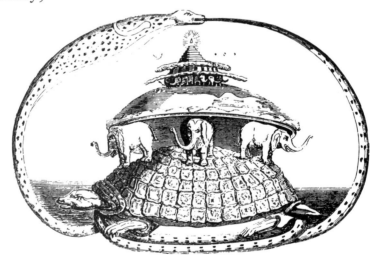

And if man is made in an image of a god,
Then the *Hathi*, the elephant, is made only in the image of an
    animal.

On the night of the birth of the Buddha
An elephant entered the dreams of Queen Mahāmāyā, his
   mother . . .
And Gautama Buddha was consequently patient, strong, meek
And unforgetful.

But when it was thought the elephant
Could best be experienced
By putting it into a forced labour camp,
Or by killing it
And packaging bits of it as billiard balls,
Umbrella stands, rosary beads,
And book-ends in its own image . . .
Then it became geared to the mass market,
Which has seen fit to reduce it to a bowdlerised
    Dumbo-Jumbo,
A performing slave in a designer cage,

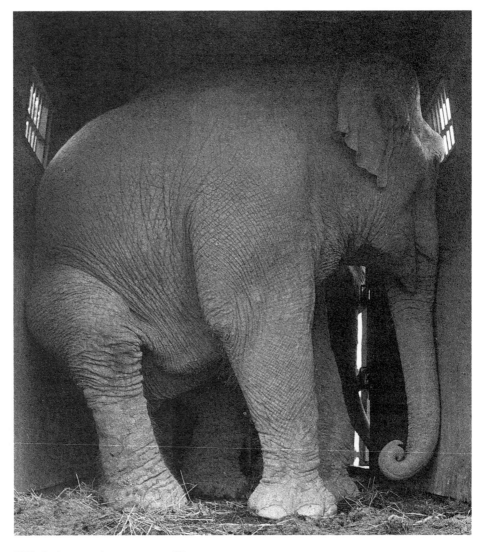

With its tusks sawn off
And a ring through a piece of flesh
Sensitive enough to read Braille.

Elephas maximus, Loxodonta africana, Elephas indicus –
To give its names in the forensic fossil-language of
    post-mortems –
Nature's blasting, billowing Archangel,
A land-manatee,
A land-siren,
A land-whale –
The oldest and largest of land mammals
Was born in the late Ice Age
While we were only a glint in Darwin's eye.

The elephant moves slowly to protect its vast brain,
With which it hears subsonic sound,
And in which it carries the topology,
The resonances and reverberations,
Of a continent.

To the elephant, our scrap of consciousness
May seem as inconsequential as a space-invader blip.

The elephant can walk on the tips of its toes
Along mountain paths that are near-vertical.
It can move in silence without leaving a trace,
And is unembarrassed by its bulk.

Though it moves at a stately pace,
It can sprint faster than any human –
Thirty to forty miles an hour –
Yet never travels so fast that it loses track of itself.
It takes two and a half days to digest its food.

It washes, massages and powders its quilted skin with fine
   dust, daily.
Its surface muscles are so cunningly tuned
That they can crush a colony of *Haematomyzus*, elephant lice,
With one focussed ripple –
Human beings
Similarly infested
Can only bleat to I.C.I.

With its ears it can discern a mouse,
Which is reassuring for mice;
And while our ears are addicted to noise –
Thrice-chewed auditory gum –
The elephant's huge sounding-boards
Open and close like eye-lids,
Excluding debilitating junk
With an enshrouding Trappist blink.
With them, it fans its whole body,
Cooling the blood by filtering it
Through needle-thin vessels,
Sailing calmly through any climate.

The trunk, through which it breathes,
The nose and upper lip,
The ringed proboscis,
With sixty thousand muscles,
Has nothing to do with baggage:
From *trompe*, trumpet,
Because that is what the rhythmic rush of air
Up and down it
Sounds like.
When it is not humming,
Or roaring,
Or piping,
Or talking,
Or purring,
Or rumbling,
Or sneezing –
The trunk can stun a dog with a sneeze.

The Aryans of the first millennium
Called the elephant *Mrigi hastin*,
The beast with a head-finger –

And with it an elephant can remove a thorn
Or pick up a pin,

Uncork a bottle,
Pull up a tree by its roots,
Detect trip-wires and traps,
Doodle in the sand,
Dowse for water underground,

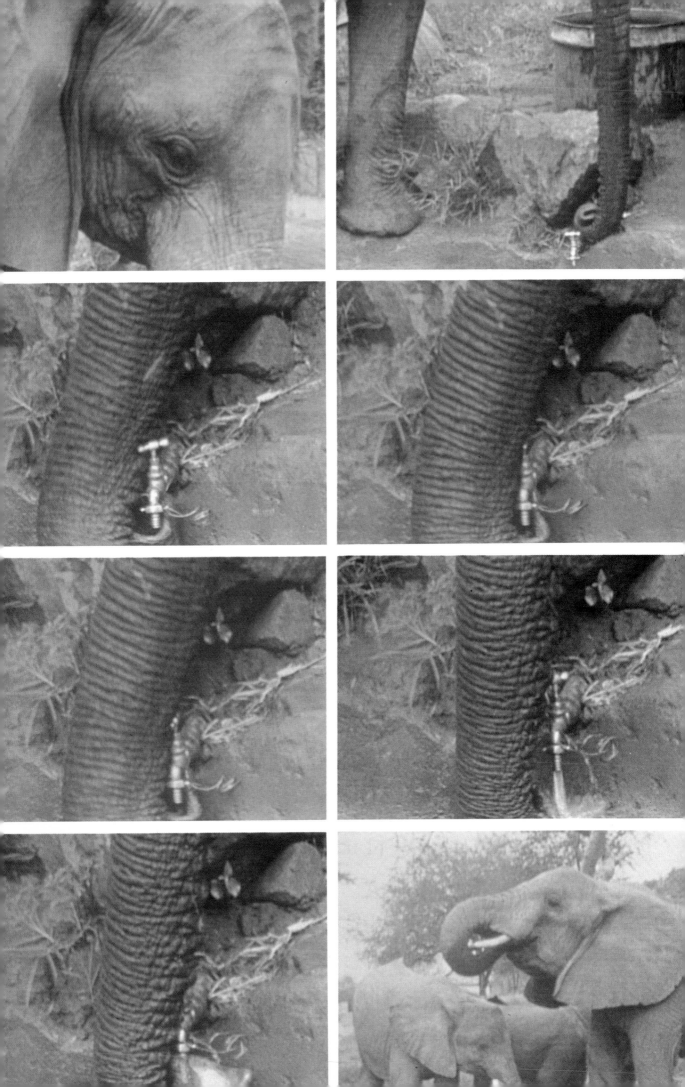

Walk along river-beds,

Swim across inland oceans,
And sense alien presences many miles away . . .

The trunk is a six-foot-long, one-foot-thick third eye –
No occultist's conceit –
Without which the elephant would starve.

When in pairs,
Elephants slowly snake their trunks
Across each other's faces to read the chemical language
Exuding from *musth* glands in their cheeks;
Then they stop, waveringly,
The tips hover and are cupped against the skin upon the
    forehead
As if picking up signals from within;
Then their trunks are disconnected,
And wreathed together in a loving knot.

Elephants' foreplay can last three days,
And that's very heavy petting –
They can show affection without being instantly possessed
By a desire to get their rocks off on the spot . . .
And their rocks are no Smarties:
One aberrant jet of elephant sperm
Will feed a forty-foot-high anthill
For a year.

Pregnancy lasts two years –
Which suggests that they've given it a thought.
There seems to be no need for the ultra-sonic scanners
Neurotically poking at a foetus half-pickled in food
    preservative,
Or the epidurals, or the monitoring devices
Of those who've lost touch with their, far smaller, bodies.
Their ante-natal care is care free.

An elephant's birth is attended by a midwife
In the centre of a protective circle.
The baby's first sight is of its placental membrane
Being tweaked into the air
And flipped away in triumphant relief
Like a giant, flailing Frisbee.

The elephant's child enters a matriarchal, communalist society
With breast milk available at every street corner.

A herd of five hundred elephants
Is a mobile crêche and an old people's home,
Where each elephant knows every fellow-member
By what it is that we glibly call 'name'.
And an elephant can detect fellow members of its tribe
From a distance of ten miles –
Human beings from only two miles,
Which makes the human aura eight miles weaker.

Elephants' tusks, their swords,
Are used mainly as ploughshares –
For breaking up chosen scraps of earth
To eat, and cure themselves of internal parasites;
For digging wells;

For finding salts and mineral crystals to fuel the brain;
For gathering food.
Neither the Cruise missile nor the Trident
Is capable of doubling up as a cocktail stick.
The adrenalin of one herd
Would keep a small war in the Middle East going for a
    month –
Elephants just dip into it occasionally,
To adjust the fine tuning within the community.

Despite the invisible intricacies of elephant society,
Some would cast them all as 'rogues',
Judging them by the notoriety of one.
Every culture has its lone delinquents,
But should you be regarded as psychotic
Simply because you have toothache,
Or because you're a male in *musth*,
Forcibly transported to a country
With no female elephants for five hundred miles,
Nor any for the rest of your life?

In the wild almost all 'rogues' are turned mad,
Blinded by tea-planters' grape-shot,
Pock-marked with septicaemic sores
From crossbow bolts dunked in battery-acid,
Or chronically disturbed by a bullet embedded in the skull.

. . . If you had roamed every continent
For thousands of years,
Coming to consider the globe your own private football,

And you were then confined to an open prison,
A tourist-infested allotment
In the suburbs of Nairobi,
On emergency rations,
You too might become unbalanced.

Rogue or sane,
Elephants are mowed down without discrimination
In an imperious cull
By the bureaucrats of ecology
Who see fit to pass judgment on them for ruining their own
    landscape,
Though elephants have felled favoured baobabs since
    antiquity,
Preferring the juicy core, rich in calcium,
To rummaging through safari-lodge dustbins.

The Nandi and the Masai know the elephant
As a survivor from an older order,
And defer to its seniority
In matters of land-tenure.

Now the domain of the elephants
Is laid waste by urban encroachment,
And their diet whittled down
From fifty different fruits in their ancestral Eden

To parched grass, and human refuse;
Accordingly they have begun to postpone puberty,
Lengthen the intervals between calving,
To slow down their breeding
And match their population to the arid nutrients that remain.
Yet conservationists presumptuously ignore the change,
And as the elephant makes its own biological adjustments,
The oldest and wisest members of the herd,
Who know their habitat far better than their killers ever
    could,
Who know the ranges, the sources of food and water,
The salt-licks, the signs of an enemy,
Are executed, leaving the herd to flounder and disperse,

Victims of military calculations
Of their own land's carrying capacity.

Their murder is described as a 'sampling'.
The elephant is shat upon with greater honesty by vultures.

Industrialists,
Who turn the Amazonian jungle into useless tundra
Or cement over half the planet,
Are not, for some reason,
Machine-gunned *en masse*,
Nor captured and exhibited,
Nor do they have their teeth extracted
And carved into little men.

Of course,
Animals don't know what is happening to them . . .
They are spared our strong emotions . . .
Yet elephants will place their trunks
Into the mouths of injured companions,
Nudge and nurse the wounded to their feet,
Knowing that their weight may press down fatally
Upon their lungs.
They will cake each other's wounds with a styptic clay
To staunch the flow of blood.
They have been known to practise mercy-killing.

They will examine corpses extensively:
Scanning the whole body,
Using the dilated tips of their trunks as organic stethoscopes
Conducting an autopsy to determine the cause of death . . .

Although there is often little mystery,
The 'Elephants' Graveyard' being a sentimental myth
Serving only to cover up the site
Of an elephant pogrom.

But when elephants are allowed to die
In their own time and space,
They will sometimes hold up a fallen body
As if forming a funeral cortège;
And bury their dead
By covering them with mud, earth, leaves and branches;

Then return later to draw the tusks,
Removing them several miles away –
Or seizing them and shattering them against a nearby tree,
As if to cheat traders,
As they have done since Herodotus recorded the ruse.

A captive elephant will perform the same last rites
Upon itself.
And from a shared aquatic past,
The elephant inherits the one quality
That *Homo sapiens* has always arrogantly assumed
Distinguishes him from the brute beast –
An elephant in distress
Will weep salt tears.

And now, in its extremity,
The elephant is breeding its ivory away:
A female elephant looking for a mate
Will choose a bull with less noticeable tusks,
As his fatherly interest in their offspring
May have a longer course to run.
If animals did not think, they would die.
Eleven feet tall and weighing six tons,
The elephant has previously paid little heed
To the human scale of things,
Remaining untroubled by its dismissal as mere animal -

A creature with the breath of life:
Anima, a breeze, then breath, then life,
Then soul.
Anima.

The elephant breathes frugally,
Only twelve times a minute,
And it can detect even odourless toxins
With the lining of its proboscis:

We, on the other hand,
Are content to breathe in anything
On the off-chance it has air in it.

The phases of an elephant's life
Run parallel to the ages of man –
With one exception:
Through its ability to lower its metabolic rate
Further than any other mammal, to an almost reptilian level,
It has the edge on man for longevity.
Its low metabolism
Enables the elephant to live up to legend
And retain its memory for longer:
All but petrifying it in a cerebral cement-mixer
Filled with sodium salts,
And immersing it slowly in giant vascular tanks
Of protein fixative . . .
Though there may still be many things
The elephant would rather forget.

Human busybodies,
Blunting box after box of scalpel blades,
Have discovered, and ghoulishly rediscovered,
That elephants' brains weigh twelve pounds
And are four times the size of ours . . .
At birth, a human being may weigh seven pounds.
An elephant baby's brain
Weighs nine.

Elephants, as nomads,
Had no cause to be defensive
Until men littered the landscape
With the upstart products of the human mind,
Which elephants address with dynamic disdain.

When they have a mind to
They will turn over hamburger stands,
Crush and grind Range-Rovers with Luddite zeal,

Uproot telephone poles,
Smash down game reserve fencing constructed of steel
    railroad tracks,
Cave in buildings,

Charge at trains dividing their land,
Tear down traffic signs,
And pulverise asphalt roads – originally elephant paths –
Until they are unusable . . .
Hannibal's tanks become eco-terrorists.

To the elephant, our solid and important artefacts
Are merely the stalking-horses of human interference –
Irritations to be cunningly disposed of,
Often under cover of darkness, guerrilla-like,
Months after the immediate affront,
As if it believes, like some Mosaic Godfather,
That revenge is a meal best eaten cold.
For until men learned to lure the elephant into traps,
It was the Lord of Creation –

A fact it may find hard to overlook.

First worshipped,
Then sacrificed . . .

Worshipped because it was the nearest thing on earth
To a cloud –
Large, grey, wafting gently across the world –
And therefore thought suited to support those
Who seem to have been touched by the celestial,
Decorated as a Brahmin,
And mounted with a temple
To contain them.

And when, in the long path of contemplation called
    Theravada,
Enlightenment was reached,
The state was depicted as the silhouette of an elephant –
Engulfed in flames,
An all-embracing presence.
A floating ball of light,
Like the power of an unconstrained mind.

The mixture of elephant and man, *Ganesha*,
The Remover of Obstacles,
Depicted a union between man and animal
That could infuse its followers with courage and prudence;
Ganesha could also bestow freedom from bad luck,
As animals are seldom observed to put a foot wrong.
In the Hindu pantheon, this elephant-headed god who
    blended the large with the small,
Macrocosm with microcosm,
Was a deity worshipped by the other gods as their teacher,
Since a glimpse of him brought happiness
And made you laugh.

In Shinto, *Baku*, a minute elephant,
Was placed beside a believer's bed,
Having the receptive power to siphon off nightmares,
Leaving the sleeper in peace.

And should the Buddha dream of returning,
It has been thought that, this time round,
His favoured incarnation
Would be as an elephant:
The strangest manifestation of life.

. . . First worshipped, then sacrificed . . .

A newer, shabbier religion –
Man alone, man maximised –
Made different demands . . .
The elephant's size seemed a challenging affront
To man's urge to see himself at the centre of things;
The elephant was a monster
Because it was larger than man;
The elephant was hunted down
And killed.
Punily prey to overblown fears,
Man concocted a temporary conquest of them
By killing something larger than himself,
Crowing over his self-assertion.

Free of carnivorous bile,
The pacific elephant was persuaded to bear arms,
To strike the same terror into the heart of an enemy.

As man moved from hunter-gatherer
To defensive agriculturalist,
The elephant became a casualty of his role-playing
And was killed for trampling down his crops.

As one tribe overran another,
The elephant became the emblem of conquest:

Its dismembered parts strewn across a continent,
As trophies,
To commemorate the penetration of two others.
In an epidemic of Boy's Own atrocity,
The teeth of the opposition's exotica were pulled:
White tusks from the two dark continents
Were displayed in suburban homes,
Each tusk the innocent agent of human slavery,
As ton after ton of ivory
Was marched through mile upon mile of bush.

Ever-obliging, the elephant was tricked
Into destroying its own habitat,
Requisitioned into transporting hardwoods
For ships and railroads.

Bought and sold,
Used to lend a second-hand sense of majesty
To its conquerors –
Grey panjandrums boxed in tawdry jewel-cases
Strapped to its back –

The elephant then became a diverting target
For bored plutocrats,
Diminished further by the patronising description:
Big game.

Forced at gun-point
To join in the game,
It was carved into convoluted knick-knacks,
Polished into cream-fleshed household gods . . .
Concentric balls, one inside another,
And then another inside that . . .
To serve as a trifling talking-point;
The miniaturised finesse of countless drawing-room
    trumperies,
Masking the mindlessness
With which the raw material was acquired
For pistol grips, painstaking baubles, bracelets,
For baroque beermugs, hairbrushes, opulent fans,
For spillikins, chess-pieces, dice-boxes and knife-handles . . .

Kitsch crucifixes,
With pale, translucent bodies hanging from them,
For the hypnotised attentions of the devout –
Too transported to see the irony
Of a scene of torture
Made of ivory
Posing as love . . .

Mannered figurines, bas-relief medallions,
Perfume flasks, snuff-boxes, shuttles,
Combs, croziers and caskets,
Pernickety furniture and art-deco fittings,
Fastidious jiggery-pokery
Prinked and pampered into 'important pieces'
By suede-voiced auctioneers
From the residually dominant class,
And sold for little fortunes
To the luxuriated . . .

Toys for rich grown-ups,
Impoverished by their dim forgetfulness:
For the image of an elephant, alive,
Could take them back to the awe of childhood
In a trice.

A vast vegetarian
Watched gravely from the sidelines
As man fought with other carnivores for meat,
Dress-rehearsing with animals
For making war upon himself . . .
The elephant comes from the Old World to the New
To be slaughtered, then snookered in safari parks,
A murder victim in the lumber room,
An incriminating witness to a buried crime.

A look in the eyes,
Hinting at some prepared testimony
Never to be delivered,

As if some record lies within
Of the extent to which its numbers
Have been ploughed into the fast-lane,
A stupendous in-fill
As man drives on.

Now peered down upon
With ungrateful detachment,
The elephant is regarded as obsolete,
Brushed aside.

A superfluous enormity,
Thick-skinned, slothful, clumsy,
Quaintly lovable,
But a ludicrous left-over
From a less useful age:
An innocent Gulliver
Snared, stranded and hemmed-in
By an expedient Lilliput.

'Sit up.
Stand up.
Stand on your head.
Take a bow.'
Look human.
Look ridiculous,
Or we'll goad you, beat you, prick you.

It might be thought that the elephant
Would be hard to humiliate,
But it has humbly allowed people to try:

By balancing on bottles,
By pushing a pram,
By sweeping the street,
By mowing lawns . . .
Used as a theatrical prop
For man to humour himself
And his denatured drudgery.

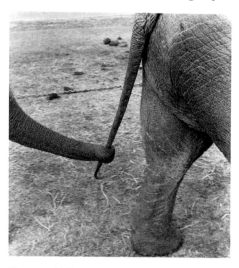

By walking round and round in circles, trunk to tail,
In an atrophied parody of the technique used
To cross rivers in safety
In an interconnected convoy.
By tossing a rubber ball up and down,
And up and down,
Instead of looping a freshly discovered melon
Into its mouth.

By rearing up on its hind legs,
As if foraging,
Only to be greeted with the fruitless rattle
Of an audience's applause
And the snorting recognition
Of a twisted anthropomorphism
As it forms neat gymnastic patterns and pyramids
In a bogus pastiche of the group consciousness
Needed to survive in the wild.
Its expansive instinct for play
Is squeezed into a couple of garish, and regimented,
Chinks in the day:
The matinée and evening performance.
The rest of its time
Spent chained and boxed
In a metal container in the circus ground,
To be considered once more
An uncouth beast,
From its odd behaviour
When caged.

Chemically immobilised in the name of pseudo-science,

The elephant may alternatively awaken
In the textured-concrete paddock of a zoo –
Its origins likewise
In the seamier side of show-business –
To be sentenced to life imprisonment
For being unusual.

Though it has no interest in the homely virtues,
It is contained in a so-called Elephant House,
So that its audience may feel cosier about its domestication.
In a last penal colony –
Facetiously oriental
Or imperiously brutal
And inauthentically rat-infested –
Besieged by tsetse-flies in human form
It is unable to swat,
The elephant moves from one foot to the other,
Shifting its confined weight, repeatedly,

For the onlooker's education in Natural History,
Its own powers of observation
Whittled down to a moribund gaze;
Its detention reducing its trunk
To an instrument with which to beg,
Comic to those who have no need to beg.

Occasionally, it will dig a hole in the concrete floor
Or impotently deface a composition rock
In a quest for the complex mineral salts
It once needed to feed its mind.

It is said that when an elephant is in trouble
Even a frog will kick it.
One small, final indignity,
The fate of all minorities,
Is for the elephant to be the butt in a rash
Of seemingly innocent,
Archly disparaging jokes . . .
'How many elephants can you get into a . . . ?'
And the answer could shortly be none.

But as they stand silently,
Imprisoned in a micro theme-park,
Surrounded by insulting paraphernalia for their 'behavioural
    enrichment',
A foot purposelessly hung in mid-air,
A limp trunk swaying like a pointless pendulum
For the amusement of evolution's latest arrival;
As they fan their ears
To waft phrases of their chemical language
Towards each other, if there is another;
And as a female dips her tail into her vagina,
Waving it back and forth through the urban air
As a scent-flag, with regal despond,
While her fellow creatures are machine-gunned
For tusks as thin as pencils,
Tweaked from their faces with chain-saws . . .
Without waiting upon the distant concerns of the
    well-intentioned
An elephant will occasionally go on the rampage,
Screaming against the obscenity of its fate.

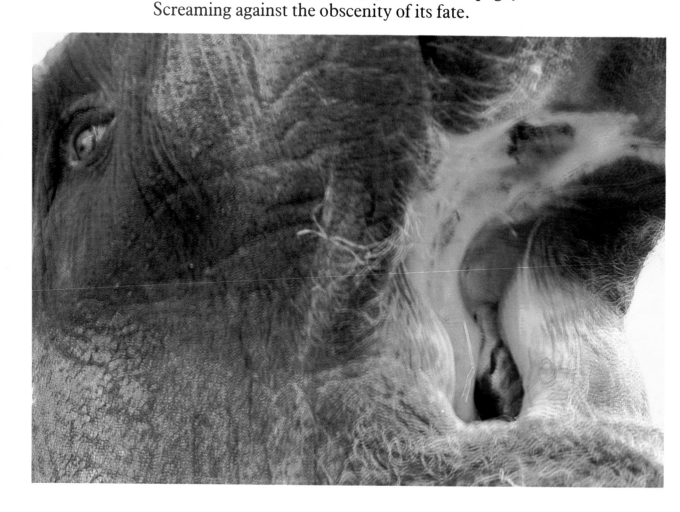

To a lone elephant in the zoo,
Humming in infra-sound
In the hope of a remote response in its infertile haven,
The final truth of its isolation
And depletion
May sometimes dawn upon it,
And it will take the law into its own hands,
Where it belongs,
And pick up its keeper,
The immediate agent of its anguish,
However benign a tyrant he has been,
Dispassionately coil its trunk around his neck,
And crack his head open against the
    wall of its cell,
Like a coconut;
Then trample the body underfoot,
And kick and scrape the remains into
    its bedding
And conceal it,
Overcome with remorse.

After years in human captivity,
Years of listening to simpering voices through the bars
Commenting upon its every move,
The elephant is required to bow
To the expectations of its proprietors.
It is consequently destroyed

By those whose high-minded notions of justice
May merely have their origins
In a nervous, haunted fear
That the spirits of slaughtered animals,
Whose corpses propped up the beginnings of their
   civilisation,
Might return to seek retribution –
Such social values
Being little more than the bonding of simian pack-animals,
Seeking to avoid a lethal squabble
While dividing up the carcass of a murdered beast;
Anxious to seek a compromise
Sealed by a mutual glow of self-approval.

Consequently, the elephant's sense of justice
Does not wait upon that of another species,
Coming as it does from another dispensation,
Older than human memory.

Like the wise child,
The elephant is born old
And looking as if already let into the great secret . . .

A sense of the other,
Which we reject,
Wanting only a sense of ourselves.

And as billiard-balls click,
Making their trivial collisions,
As the lager flows,
Who knows what resonates in the aether,
Unresolved . . . ?

An ivory worker, in New York,
Once contracted anthrax
While making piano keys,
Inhaling the dust
With its traces of the infection
From which the elephant he was re-forming
Had died . . .
As if something marched to a different drummer,
And there was a more scrupulous notation
Than that guiding human hands
Across ivory keys, in heedless elation.

Elephants suffer from the same diseases as man,
And share the same emotions:
Love, rage, hate, envy, pride,
Exhilaration, and despair . . .

Captured and tied up for hours in logging camps,
An elephant will commit suicide.

Threatened, and attacked by overwhelming odds,
It will place itself in the line of fire,
Dying in the cause of a greater good,
Protecting its fellow creatures, or its young,
Brought to an end by those to whom it is expedient
To think that the elephant has a diminished awareness of
    death;
Killed by those it may regard, in turn,
As rogue humans.

If Buddha, Lao Tzu and the Nazarene were not quite men,
Then it is just as likely that some elephants
Were not quite elephants:
That long ago, in an elephant dreamtime,
Some spiritual counterpart amongst them
First took the love of its own kind
To an unprecedented extreme,
Its memory lingering productively
In their tribal consciousness . . .
The first altruist.

But who are we to know?
Fallen out of love with our own kind,
Persistently killing those who have not,
Turning them into butchered blobs,
Carving their bones with mercenary fetishism,
Until the elephant becomes no more than a memory.

It is through an excited compulsion to learn the names of
     animals
That a child first learns to speak.
'Elephant!'
The word is pronounced with magnetic recognition.
'Elephant!'
A large and germinative being
With whom the child gains a sense of the diversity
Of its own creature feelings, as yet unformed;
Sharpens its wits, structures its thought:
'As big as an elephant . . . Just like an elephant . . .'
Through using animals
As metaphor, as simile, as allegory;
Through making sense of the ambiguous borderland
Of the non-human;
Through puzzling out a world that could produce elephants,
The child gains the notion
Of another state of play
Nearer the roots of creation.

In the last decade
Six out of ten of the elephants in Africa
Have been massacred;
And the entire population
May soon be shovelled contemptuously
Into the realm of mythology.

In the mind's eye of a child
An elephant
Should now be more accurately depicted
As a mutilated corpse.

Through mimicry, through games,
Through trying different moulds before maturing,
And playing with other identities than its own,
The child has shaped its world
And slowly become human.

Once the child grows up
The elephant may be abandoned and forgotten
As if it were little more than a frivolous ghost.

But until then
It is a touchstone of the child's imagination,
One of the first images of the world
Alerting the child to its wonder.

Pictures and models of animals
Are latched on to tenaciously,
For by entering another domain
The child suspends its small, confined reality,
Widens the range of the perennial question 'Who am I?'
And prepares an escape route
From the exhausting, centrifugal force of human domination.
In that other region, there are creatures larger and stronger
    than its parents,
With a different authority.

In collaboration with their distant disposition,
A sense of their gathered power,
The child's awareness expands,
Before its attention is turned away
From the animal to the machine;
Before its passage is forced into a man-made society
With its elephantine surrogates:
Tower blocks, juggernauts and trampling multinationals,
Monster markets, jumbo jets, and motorways . . .
Before it is crushed by the elephantiasis of technology,
Where there is less and less room for any mammals
Larger than rats.
And where, henceforth, the elephant may exist
Only in a scratched nature-film,
A destitute freak in a video zoo,

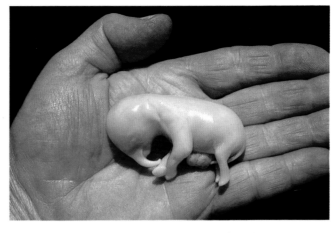

This large link in the chain of being
Broken beyond repair . . .
One of the happiest ingredients of a child's psyche
Withered, and amputated.
'Elephant!'
The word will be exclaimed with its familiar magic,
But there may be no more elephants.

Through the living bodies of animals
We gain an inkling of how things came to be.
As their dead bodies pile up
We are merely jostled towards our end,
Our fate being joined to theirs
In an alliance we cannot bear to acknowledge.

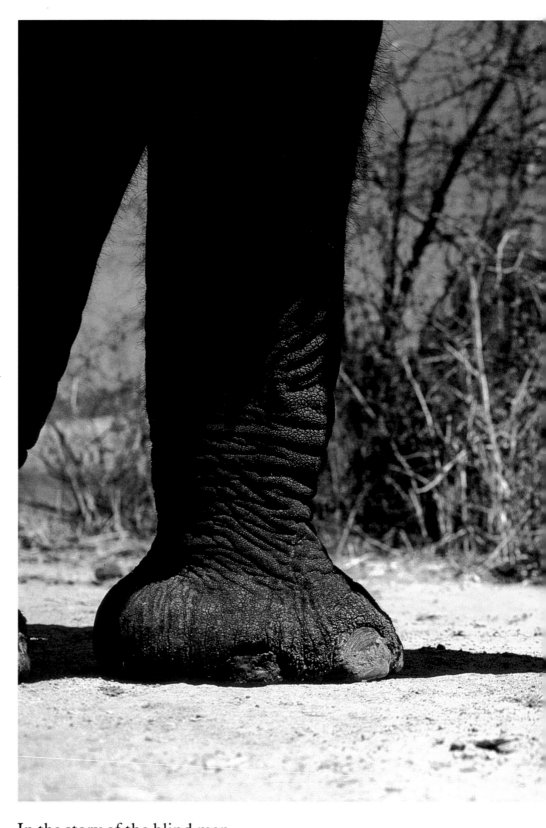

In the story of the blind men,
Each one gave a different description of the elephant,
Depending upon which part of it he felt.
Now they are to be left
Feeling only each other.

On the Nature of Elephants

In the beginning of all things, wisdom and knowledge were with the animals; for Tirawa, the One Above, did not speak directly to man. He sent certain animals to tell men that he showed himself through the beasts, and that from them, and from the stars and the sun and the moon, man should learn. Tirawa spoke to man through his works.

Chief Letakots-Lesa of the Pawnee Tribe, in Natalie Curtis, *The Indians' Book: An Offering by the American Indians of Indian Lore, Musical and Narrative, to Form a Record of the Songs and Legends of Their Race*, New York: Harper & Brothers, 1907

The two kinds of living elephants are the only survivors of a huge order of animals, with no fewer than 352 different branches, which during the past sixty million years has been spread over almost the whole land surface . . .

Richard Carrington, *Elephants*, London: Chatto & Windus, 1958

The elephant's heart is peculiar, in that its apex presents two points instead of one like most mammals. This peculiarity is however shared by certain whales, dugong, etc.

G. H. Evans, *Elephants and Their Diseases: A Treatise on Elephants*, Rangoon, Burma: Government Printing, 1910

The concept of once-terrestrial animals having returned to the sea is a very familiar one. The concept that an animal, having once made that transition, might subsequently return to the land and re-adapt to terrestrial life is unfamiliar, but in evolutionary terms there is nothing intrinsically unacceptable about it.

There is one other animal which bears many of the hallmarks of having made the double transition – very much earlier than the aquatic ape. The aquatic theory does not stand or fall by the proposition that the elephant is another example of an ex-aquatic animal, but there are many features of his physiology and behaviour which would support such a hypothesis.

(1) Like many aquatic mammals he is virtually hairless, except for a tuft on his tail and sometimes a patch of hair on his head. Some extinct forms, such as the mammoth which inhabited mainly sub-Arctic environments, possessed a hairy coat; and the young of the present-day elephants are born covered with yellow and brown hair which is later shed – possibly analogous to the lanuginous coat of the human foetus.

(2) Elephants have webbing between their toes.

(3) The vaginal canal of the female elephant follows a route unknown in any other terrestrial mammal [see below]. It emerges in such an unusual position that it used to be believed that elephants copulated ventro-ventrally.

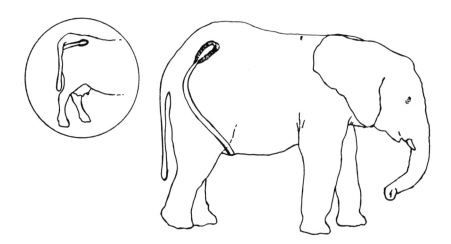

(4) Carcases of mammoths have more than once been found in the Arctic completely preserved by the ice. A subcutaneous layer of fat about 8 centimetres thick covered the whole body.

(5) The elephant's penis, like the whale's, is completely retractable into a special pocket in the body wall. In the case of the whale the purpose is to provide streamlining.

(6) The opening in the skull for the nostrils has migrated dorsally, as with whales and other marine mammals: it emerges above the eyes. This is not readily observable because in the soft tissue the air canal thereafter continues downwards and emerges at the end of the trunk.

(7) The diaphragm is oblique, as in whales and dugongs.

(8) The elephant is an excellent swimmer. He has been known of his own volition to swim distances of up to 300 miles to offshore islands.

(9) He sheds tears when emotionally disturbed.

(10) He has voluntary control of vocal utterances: elephants can easily be trained to trumpet to order.

(11) When an elephant gives birth, another female (popularly described as a 'midwife elephant') stands by until the process is complete. The *Encyclopaedia Britannica* attributes this to defence against predators. 'In regions where large carnivores such as tigers prey upon newborn elephants, the cow seeks a female associate.' However, it would take a very brave or hungry lion to approach a 5-ton elephant in labour closely enough to snatch away her baby. The 'female associate' is strongly reminiscent of the dolphin midwife who stays near to assist the newborn to the surface for its first breath. This behaviour is known in no other terrestrial species, with the exception of our own.

The evolution of tusks has never been satisfactorily explained. They occur in several mammalian species which are totally unrelated to one another. These species include – apart from the elephant and its extinct relatives – the walrus, the sea cow and the babirussa. All have naked hides and all are either aquatics or swamp dwellers.

Elaine Morgan, *The Aquatic Ape: A Theory of Human Evolution*, London: Souvenir Press, 1982

Ethiopia produces elephants that rival those of India . . . The Ethiopian tribe in whose country they are chiefly bred are called the Asachaeans; it is stated that in coast districts belonging to this tribe the elephants link themselves four or five together into a sort of raft and holding up their heads to serve as sails are carried on the waves to the better pastures of Arabia.

Pliny the Elder, *Natural History*, VIII, 35

With the exception of the whale, it [the elephant] is probably the finest swimmer of all the mammals.

Reginald Campbell, *Teak-Wallah: The Adventures of a Young Englishman in Thailand in the 1920s*, London: Hodder & Stoughton, 1935

During a trek across the largest island of the Northern group [of the Andaman Islands], I was amazed to discover the tracks and droppings of an elephant which I could only suppose was a wild one. Judging from the impressions of the pads and the size of the droppings, I came to the conclusion that it was a young animal, about twenty years old. I got quite close to him on two occasions, but, owing to the dense jungle, was unable to see him before he winded me. Thus I was left guessing, until the end of our exploring trip.

My inquiries then revealed that a seven-year-old calf elephant, one of the South Andaman Forest Department's elephants, had been missing twelve years before. It had been 'written off' in the Forest Department records as 'believed drowned', having been seen attempting to swim from island to island. The age of this animal coincided pretty well with my estimate, and there can be no doubt it was the same. It was a remarkable swim, for it was over 200 miles from where he was last seen to where I found him, and some of his swims from island to island must have been at least a mile in the open sea, which is seldom without a swell, and in a country where there are two monsoons a year. Of course, he had twelve years in which to do it, and no doubt he had a good sojourn on each island before moving to the next.

J. H. Williams, *Elephant Bill*, London: Rupert Hart-Davis, 1950

The presence of fossil elephants on certain islands off California, in the Mediterranean, in Indonesia, and off China, has led to two widely accepted assumptions: (1) that elephants, being poor swimmers, could not have swum to the islands and therefore must have walked to them, which indicates that (2) land bridges once joined the islands to the mainland. These two assumptions have profoundly influenced various insular biogeographic and geologic reconstructions on and around these islands. New evidence, however, shows unequivocally that living elephants are excellent distance swimmers. They swim in a lunging, porpoise-like fashion while using their trunk as a snorkel. Elephant swimming speeds have been measured up to 2.70 km/h, and maximum distances estimated at 48 km. Their chief motives for swimming seem to be that they can see the islands and smell food on them.

Donald Lee Johnson, 'Problems in the land vertebrate zoogeography of certain islands and the swimming powers of elephants', *Journal of Biogeography*, 7, 383–98, Oxford: Blackwell Scientific Publications, 1980

If necessary, they [elephants] will swim through the larger [Chad] lakes, some of them as big as a thousand to three thousand square yards. It is a wonderful sight to see two hundred elephants, old and young, diving and swimming with great elegance, only the tops of their big heads showing . . .

H. Oberjohann, *Komoon: Capturing the Chad Elephant*, New York: Pantheon, 1952

It may be recalled that when Hannibal crossed the Rhine in Europe some of the elephant rafts overturned and, although some of the attendants were drowned, the African elephants in spite of their heavy foot chains *swam* ashore 'with great churning of the water'.

Sylvia K. Sikes, *The Natural History of the African Elephant*, London: Weidenfeld & Nicolson, 1971

Elephants definitely are water-loving animals and in some areas, where conditions dictate or permit, they actually follow a semi-aquatic way of life, which probably reflects the semi-aquatic life-style of their ancestors; manatees and sea cows are among the closest living relatives of the elephant. The evolution of the trunk and the absence of a pleural cavity in elephants may also reflect the semi-aquatic habits of their ancestors. The spongy character of the elephant's skull with its innumerable air cavities may be an adaptation to minimise skull weight as well as provide buoyancy in water. Further, elephants regularly need water to bathe, presumably to keep cool and to maintain their physiological well being.

Donald Lee Johnson, 'Problems in the land vertebrate zoogeography of certain islands and the swimming powers of elephants', *Journal of Biogeography*, 7, 383–98, Oxford: Blackwell Scientific Publications, 1980

Full grown elephants swim perhaps better than any other land animals. A batch of seventy-nine that I despatched from Dacca to Barrackpur, near Calcutta, in November, 1875, had the Ganges and several of its large tidal branches to cross. In the longest swim they were six hours without touching the bottom; after a rest on a sand-bank, they completed the swim in three more; not one was lost. I have heard of more remarkable swims than this.

G. P. Sanderson, *Thirteen Years Among the Wild Beasts of India*, London: W. H. Allen, 1878

The secret of the elephant's ancestry was discovered by palaeontologists some years ago in the Fayoum beds in the Egyptian Desert. In these beds of Tertiary age were found the remains of animals related to modern elephants, but less than half their size, which had a short proboscis or trunk as indicated by the abbreviated nasal bones. Besides possessing a trunk, the elephant has a peculiar tooth arrangement or type of succession in his grinding or cheek teeth as they are often called. The teeth do not fit into permanent sockets or cavities in the jaw bones, as teeth do in other mammals. Instead, they pass through the jaws from behind forward. In other words, as they wear out, the teeth behind push the worn ones out of the jaw and take their place.

The only other group of mammals in which teeth pass thus through the jaws are the manatees. And, oddly enough, in the Fayoum beds of Egypt have been

found remains of mammals intermediate between elephants and manatees. These fossil manatee-like animals imply a common ancestry for the two groups which are today widely diverse in anatomy and habits. The manatees are almost as thoroughly aquatic as whales and live in the water where they spend most of their time submerged feeding on grasses and other vegetation growing on the bottoms of lakes and large rivers. As the manatee rises above the surface of the water to breathe, its rounded head gives it a very human appearance. They are very shy animals and difficult to approach closely in a boat. Sailors seeing manatees at a distance have, it is thought, invented the tales regarding the existence of mermaids. Who would have ever thought that Science would trace the elephant back to a mermaid ancestry?

Edmund Heller, 'Elephants In and Out of the Zoo', *Bulletin of the Washington Park Zoological Society of Milwaukee*, May 1933

The beast that passeth all others in wit and mind . . . and by its intelligence, it makes as near an approach to man as matter can approach spirit.

Aristotle, *De Rerum Natura*

There is not any creature so capable of understanding as an Elephant. They are apt to learne, remember, meditate, and conceive such things as a man can hardly perform.

Edward Topsell, *The History of Four-Footed Beasts, describing the True and Lively Figure of every Beast . . . collected out of all the Volumes of C. Gesner and all other Writers of the Present Day*, London: W. Jaggard, 1607

And the upper jaw from its lip has a long, ex-osseous, crooked and serpent-like protuberance; and these by nature are perforated all the way to the lungs, so as to form a double tube, so that the animal uses this pipe as a nostril for respiration, and likewise for a hand; for it could take a cup if it please with this protuberance, and can grasp it round and hold it firmly, and none could take it by force from the animal, except another stronger elephant.

Amyntianus, 'Concerning Elephants', from Book VIII, *On Cures*, (known only through Pindar, *Odes*, III, 52)

'**6**0,000 muscles manipulate it [the trunk] . . .

Margaret Lewis, 'Of the kingdom of Abu', *Dinny's Calgary Digest*, Calgary Zoological Society, 1: 7, 19–23, 1971

Next to bulk, the elephant's most distinctive feature is its trunk. This is simply a very much elongated upper lip, composed of flesh and muscle, and is as necessary to the elephant as a hand is to a human being. Kipling described in the *Just So Stories* how the Elephant's Child found his trunk a most useful instrument for chastising his relations, and a playful elephant can certainly use it to administer a hefty whack. But the trunk is not normally used for aggressive purposes, being far too sensitive and valuable an organ to be exposed to possible danger. It functions mainly as a kind of fifth limb for bringing food and water to the mouth, or collecting dust and sand to throw over its owner's body. It also plays a part in producing some of the characteristic sounds by which elephants express their wants and feelings. The blood-curdling scream of rage, imperfectly described as 'trumpeting', is the sound most commonly associated with elephants in the popular imagination, but their range of emotional expression is much wider than this. G. P. Sanderson in *Thirteen Years Among the Wild Beasts of India*, published in 1878, has described a peculiar noise made with the trunk which seems to express dislike or apprehension, and which he likens to a large sheet of tin being rapidly doubled. 'It is produced', he writes, 'by rapping the end of the trunk smartly on the ground, a current of air, hitherto retained, being sharply emitted through the trunk, as from a valve, at the moment of impact.' The trunk is also used for making squeaks of pleasure, as when domestic elephants have been separated at work all day and meet each other again in the evening. On the other hand, the low, rumbling sound expressive of want or pain is made in the throat, the trunk being raised or lowered according to the intensity of feeling.

Richard Carrington, *Elephants*, London: Chatto & Windus, 1958

If an elephant's trunk is seriously injured it will die of starvation, since everything it eats has to be torn down or pulled up and handled by the trunk.

J. H. Williams, *Elephant Bill*, London: Rupert Hart-Davis, 1950

The nostrils have evolved with the [upper] lip, and their external orifices are to be found at the tip of the trunk. This makes it possible for the elephant to determine at once by its acute sense of smell whether an object is edible or not . . . the single or double processes [single in the case of the Indian elephant, double in the African] at the end of the trunk, combined with a little suction, enable the elephant to pick up objects as small and thin as a halfpenny . . . The processes have in addition an important tactile function. Their nerves can transmit messages to the brain concerning the shape, texture, temperature, and so on, of any object touched. The hairs on the shaft of the trunk . . . also have this function, and contribute greatly to the organ's sensitivity. There are several other functions of the trunk, such as its ability to direct a stream of water at anyone its owner dislikes . . .

Richard Carrington, *Elephants*, London: Chatto & Windus, 1958

In the dry months of the year, adult elephants dig holes in dry, sandy river beds to search for subsurface water. When the herd moves off, other species, taking advantage of the holes the elephants have made, come down to drink.

John Hanks, *A Struggle for Survival: The Elephant Problem*, London: Country Life Books, 1979

'I had seen a herd of elephants travelling through dense native forest, pacing along as if they had an appointment at the end of the world.'

Karen Blixen, *Out of Africa*, London: The Bodley Head 1937

Scattered herds drift as a whole in the same direction. They close up to rest and when alarmed, at which times the females and young bunch together while the bulls move off. When first disturbed, they all fall silent and then move off swiftly without making a sound. Their normal speed is about three miles an hour, but they can make four or even five miles per hour and keep it up for ten miles. During a stampede, elephants can increase their speed to fifteen miles per hour for short distances. In a charge, loxodonts can make twenty-five miles an hour and overtake the best human runners on open level ground. The best human sprinters make twenty-two miles per hour over 100 to 200 yards, fifteen miles per hour over one mile.

Ivan T. Sanderson, *The Dynasty of Abu: A History and Natural History of the Elephants and Their Relatives Past and Present*, London: Cassell, 1960

Elephants migrate considerable distances, but the reason for this has not yet been fully explained . . . they can tolerate a wide range of temperature, so seasonal changes in climate can have little to do with their movements. The obvious explanation that they follow the supply of food and drink is not in itself sufficient, for even when both these necessities of life are present they will still readily shift their terrain. Another suggestion is that the migrations are based not so much on the general supply of food as on the seasonal availability of certain plants of which the animals are particularly fond. For instance, Stockley [Charles Hugh Stockley, 'The Elephant in Kenya', in Rowland Ward (ed.), *The Elephant in East Central Africa*, London and Nairobi, Rowland Ward Ltd, 1953] has suggested that the elephant migrates to the higher slopes of Mount Kenya in January and February because of the supply of berries of the *mukaita* tree (*Raponæa rhododendroides*) to be found there at this season. These are much sought after by the local Africans as a cure for stomach ailments, and Stockley believes the elephant may also find them of medicinal value.

Richard Carrington, *Elephants*, London: Chatto & Windus, 1958

Elephants . . . prepare medicines for the females when they are sick or in labour pains, and crowd round about them.

Abu al-Fazl ibn Mubarak (called 'Allami'), *Ain i Akbari*, translated from the Persian by H. Blochmann and H. S. Jarrett, Calcutta, 1873

When pierced by missiles, the elephant eats the flower of the olive or the actual oil and is then able to shake out the missiles and is well again.

Aelian, *De Natura Animalium*, II, 18

One might think that the elephant would indiscriminately stuff down anything and everything in reach, but the elephant is a selective feeder and its diet is extremely varied, including such exotic foods as desert dates, wild celery, black plums, wild ginger, the Shea butternut, wild olives and figs, wild coffee berries, and wild raspberries. There are some foods that elephants will not eat at all and others that they will eat only during certain times of the year or at certain growth stages.

Cynthia Moss, *Portraits in the Wild: Animal Behaviour in East Africa*, London: Hamish Hamilton, 1976

Elephants always show great discrimination in the matter of food. They prefer browsing to grazing, and are particularly fond of green leaves and the tender shoots of leguminous plants; they also eat twig ends and the soft bark of young trees, tearing the latter off with their tusks and then putting them into their mouths with their trunks. On the occasions when they graze

they naturally prefer the lush green grass that springs up after the rains, and eat dry grass and hay from necessity rather than choice. It is amusing to watch grazing elephants select a large lump of the best grass they can see, pull it up by the roots with their trunks, and then knock the loose earth against their knees before tucking it into their mouths . . .

Apart from their staple diet of green food, elephants are very partial to salt. They will travel many miles to a good salt lick, where they sweep up the salt in their trunks with every appearance of satisfaction. Coconuts are regarded as a special delicacy, and when they are ripe on the wild palms the elephants will congregate in the region and live on them for weeks. They first dispose of the fruit that has already dropped, and then encourage a further supply by butting the trees with their foreheads or shaking them with their trunks, rather as small boys obtain succulent apples when raiding orchards. They break the coconut open by pressing it gently with one of their fore-feet, and it is interesting to see how nicely they calculate the pressure so that the husk and shell are broken open without crushing their contents. The roots of the young palms are also regarded as a delicacy . . .

No elephant can resist mangoes, plantain stems, maize, or sugar cane, and they often wander onto cultivated land in search of these delicacies.

Richard Carrington, *Elephants*, London: Chatto & Windus, 1958

Elephants are not generally known for their subterranean habits, but there is one place on earth where they regularly venture deep underground . . . and that is on Mount Elgon, a vast, dormant volcano straddling the Kenya–Uganda border.

Elgon's forested valleys conceal numbers of unusual caves, cul-de-sacs that extend more or less horizontally into the mountain, frequently screened by a cascade of water.

It has long been known that elephants visit these caves and scrape the walls with their tusks. They were assumed to be in search of mineral salts or shelter . . .

We monitored the use of the cave by animals for several days and nights and on three memorable occasions witnessed elephants feeling their way underground by moonlight . . .

The study was full of surprises. One might suppose that if an elephant were to enter a dark, dangerous place full of pitfalls, it would choose the brightest time of day, avoid the dark zone of the cave and stay only as long as necessary. Observations proved just the opposite. Most visits began at dusk when whole herds of cows and calves might materialize from the gloom of the forest and slowly disappear in single file into the black maw of Kitum Cave.

They would penetrate the full 160m length of the cave and sometimes spend six hours or more, apparently at ease, in the Stygian blackness. There, by the dim light of a pen torch, I watched them groping around slabs of rock bigger than themselves, with trunks held out like built-in white canes . . .

The key to the understanding of this unique phenomenon is geophagy – the ingestion of earth or rock.

All animals have a physiological need for sodium ions; they usually get these from salts, such as sodium chloride, which occur naturally in their diet. In areas of high rainfall, however, sodium salts are leached from the soil; if the underlying rock is also devoid of salts, then herbivores feeding on the plants that grow there will somehow have to make up that deficit. They do this by visiting outcrops of mineral rich strata to lick salt . . .

The situation on Mount Elgon is similar except that the best source of sodium is in the caves. It is the universal hunger for salt that drives the elephants . . . into those dark, subterranean salt licks.

Analysis of rock samples and 10 elephant food plants confirmed this; volcanic agglomerate from the cave walls was found to contain more than 100 times the level of sodium present in the plants . . . most of the sodium is bound up in sodium sulphate (mirabilite), crystals of which grow from certain rock faces . . .

Ian Redmond, 'The underground tusk force . . . how the elephant makes himself the salt of the earth and created the great caves of Mt Elgon', London: *Guardian*, 26 January 1984

From time to time it takes to swallowing stones.

Aristotle, *Historia Animalium*, VIII, 605[a]23

Another crystal, found as perpendicular glassy needles lining cavities in the rock, is natrolite (sodium aluminium silicate) – one of the family of minerals known as zeolites. Their presence in an elephant's diet raises some intriguing possibilities.

In recent years considerable interest has been shown in the agricultural applications of zeolites. Japanese farmers have long used zeolitic tuffs [fragments of volcanic rock], as a dietary supplement for livestock. Controlled trials in both Japan and the US have demonstrated that pigs, chickens and ruminants can all benefit from the addition of up to 10 per cent zeolite to their diet.

Positive effects include the prevention and curing of digestive complaints, increased growth rates, improved feed conversion rates, lack of offensive odours from excrement and the prevention of mould in stored feed. It sounds like some sort of universal panacea for domestic animals but it may also explain some incidences of geophagy in the wild. Perhaps the herbivores visiting Elgon's caves are getting more than a simple dose of salts – the rock may also act as a tonic and an aid to digestion.

If this is the case, it may help to explain the surprising quantities of rock sometimes consumed. Forty-five per cent of dung piles examined at random in the forest contained particles of rock, ranging from grit to lumps 4cm long. On one occasion I sat on some freshly fallen roof in Kitum, watching a very tolerant bull stuffing himself with bits of broken rock for more than an hour. Every few seconds his trunk would carry a piece to his mouth and the crunch of giant molars grinding rock was clearly audible. It was impossible to gauge precisely how much he ate but it must have amounted to a couple of shovelsful.

Ian Redmond, 'The underground tusk force . . . how the elephant makes himself the salt of the earth and created the great caves of Mt Elgon', London: *Guardian*, 26 January 1984

Elephants are delighted above measure with sweet savours, ointments and smelling flowers, for which cause their keepers will in the summer-time lead them into meadows of flowers, and, by the quickness of their smelling, the elephants will themselves choose and gather the sweetest flowers and put them in baskets if the keepers have any. The baskets being filled, the elephants desire to wash themselves, like dainty and neat men, and so they will go and seek water to wash, and then of their own accord they return to the baskets of flowers. If they do not find them, they will bray and call for them. Afterward, having been led into their stable, they will not eat until their keepers take the flowers and dress the brims of their mangers with them and likewise strew their room or standing-place with them. Then they please themselves with their food because of the savour of the flowers stuck about their cratch, being like dainty fed persons who set their dishes with green herbs.

Edward Topsell, *The History of Four-Footed Beasts, describing the True and Lively Figure of every Beast . . . collected out of all the Volumes of C. Gesner and all other Writers of the Present Day*, London: W. Jaggard, 1607

They feed on the bushy mastic tree, the tender leaves of the date palm and the more sappy shoots of other plants.

Aelian, *De Natura Animalium*, VII, 6

They frequent the country from the Pongolo northward, during the summer season . . . The time of their arrival is simultaneous with the ripening of the fruit of the umganu-tree, of which they are passionately fond, and doubtless come in search of. This fruit is capable of being made into a strong intoxicating drink, and the elephants after eating it become quite tipsy, staggering about, playing huge antics, screaming so as to be heard miles off, and not seldom having tremendous fights.

W. H. Drummond, *The Large Game and Natural History of South and South-east Africa*, Edinburgh: Hamilton, 1875

One of the most unusual records I have come across of stomach contents was given to me by Roger Short. In 1965, a young male elephant lived on the Mweya Peninsula in Uganda, and for some time was known to raid the dustbins of the houses at night. Eventually the animal had to be shot, and an examination of its stomach revealed, among other items, broken glass, beer bottle tops, nuts, bolts, fish bones, a 50-cent piece, one ½-ounce weight, a sardine tin opener, the heel of a shoe, two six-inch nails, a collection of stones, the base of a light bulb, and tin foil from wine bottles.

John Hanks, *A Struggle for Survival: The Elephant Problem*, London: Country Life Books, 1979

The eyelids furnished with eyelashes blink every few seconds . . . a gland situated on the inner side of the orbit, called the Harderian gland, pours its secretions on to the third eyelid, whence the tears so produced fall onto the face.

G. H. Evans, *Elephants and Their Diseases: A Treatise on Elephants*, Rangoon, Burma: Government Printing, 1910

The Indian elephant is said sometimes to weep. Sir E. Tennent, in describing those which he saw captured and bound in Ceylon, says, some 'lay motionless on the ground, with no other indication of suffering than the tears which suffused their eyes and flowed incessantly.' Speaking of another elephant, he says, 'When overpowered and made fast, his grief was most affecting; his violence sank to utter prostration, and he lay on the ground, uttering choking cries, with tears trickling down his cheeks.' In the Zoological Gardens the keeper of the Indian elephants positively asserts that he has several times seen tears rolling down the face of the old female, when distressed by the removal of the young one.

Charles Darwin, *The Expression of the Emotions in Man and Animals*, revised and abridged by Surgeon Rear-Admiral C. M. Beadnell, London: Watts & Co., The Thinker's Library, 1934

Having planted a bullet in the shoulder-bone of an elephant, and caused the agonised creature to lean for support against a tree, I proceeded to brew some coffee. Having refreshed myself, taking observations of the elephant's spasms and writhings between the sips, I resolved to make experiments on vulnerable points, and approaching very near, I fired several bullets at different parts of his enormous skull. He only acknowledged the shots by a salaam-like movement of his trunk, with the point of which he gently touched the wounds with a striking and peculiar action. Surprised and shocked to find I was only prolonging the suffering of the noble beast, which bore his trials with such dignified composure, I resolved to finish the proceedings with all possible despatch, and accordingly opened fire on him from the left side. Aiming at the shoulder I fired six shots with the two-grooved rifle, which must have eventually proved mortal, after which I fired six shots at the same part with the Dutch six-pounder. Large tears now trickled down from his eyes, which he slowly shut and opened, his colossal frame quivered convulsively, and falling on his side he expired.

Gordon Cummings, quoted in Mark Twain, *More Tramps Abroad*, London: Chatto & Windus, 1897

It is unusual to see tears running from eyes of wild elephants, although it is common in captive specimens . . .

Sylvia K. Sikes, *The Natural History of the African Elephant*, London: Weidenfeld & Nicolson, 1971

Once upon a time, we are told in the biography of a man who spent most of his life with elephants, there were eight elephants and two men in a large building in a place called Lancaster, Missouri. The youngest, a female named Sadie, apparently just could not understand what was required of her during a course of training for forthcoming circus performances. The two men were professionals of long experience in this exacting business. They were good men but hard-boiled; their work was difficult, and they knew, or thought they knew, its every aspect. But, as one of them told his biographer, they still had something to learn about these marvellous creatures. What happened was this.

Sadie finally gave up and tried to run out of the training ring. The men ordered her back and began to 'punish' her – which, I would like to stress once again, does not entail any cruelty in such circumstances – for her supposed stupidity and for trying to run away. At this, Sadie sank to her knees and then lay down on her side, and the two men, as the chronicler records, 'stood dumbfounded for a few moments,' for Sadie was crying like a human being. 'She lay there on her side, the tears streaming down her face and sobs racking her huge body.'

In almost half a century of close association with elephants, including and even after reading a substantial part of the vast literature concerning these majestic creatures, I have not encountered anything that has moved me so greatly, and I write this in all seriousness and humility. Its ineffable pathos constantly brings to mind that most famous verse 'Jesus wept' (John 11, 35). What on earth are we to make of a so-called 'lower animal' crying?

If you shoot an animal, you may expect it to make whimpering noises, even if only as a result of mechanical reaction. Other purely physical stimuli may well cause animals to sweat – if they have the necessary cutaneous glands – or even to emit drops of liquid from their tear glands; but these are purely reflex actions. That any animal, and especially one weighing 3 tons, should lie down and sob her heart out in pure emotional frustration is something else again. It almost looks as if, despite all that we like to believe, we humans are not the only creatures that possess what we call emotions and higher feelings. In fact, if we insist upon making a distinction between ourselves and other animals in this respect, we will then have to provide a special niche for the elephants.

Ivan T. Sanderson, *The Dynasty of Abu: A History and Natural History of the Elephants and Their Relatives Past and Present*, London: Cassell, 1960

'Have you ever seen "Rani" cry?'
    'Can't say we take any notice of that.'

Robert Raven, elephant handler, Gerry Cottle's Circus, in conversation with Heathcote Williams, Plymouth, 17 September 1988

This marvel also have I heard, that the mighty Elephants have a prophetic soul within their breasts . . .

Oppian, *Cynegetica*, II, 529–55

On the march they go in single file and the leader, finding any grass that betrays the presence of man, pulls it up and gives it to the one behind to smell; it is then passed down the line to the rearmost elephant who then trumpets. At this signal they all turn aside to safer ground, always avoiding land that has been trodden by men.

Aelian, *De Natura Animalium*, IX, 56

Elephants were not so sensitive to the threat of water, perhaps because they had less to fear. But they certainly reacted quickly enough to the threat of fire. They knew even better than men that forest streams were God's fire-lines, and hearing the crackle of a forest fire they would put a stream between them and it as soon as possible, yet it seemed with no hurry.

When there were tropical storms, elephants would avoid certain forest canopies. Moving to open ground and well away from trees, they would stand without a movement of ears, trunk or tails, their eyes half-closed, waiting for the flash of lightning descending the green tree and then for the crack of thunder, their bodies drawn up in tension.

J. H. Williams, *Bandoola*, London: Rupert Hart-Davis, 1953

The elephant story was told me by the late Peter Finch, after he had been filming in 'Elephant Walk'. Elephants were required to run amok and charge through a specially constructed house – sections and furniture made to collapse easily. Apparently they were reluctant to move in but were eventually goaded. Then the lead elephant spotted a box of Swan Vestas on the floor and stalled; they stopped their rampage and gently stepped over the matches and made their way out of the house without doing *any* damage.

Alec Guinness, in a letter to Heathcote Williams, 3 September 1988

In the jungles of India the writer frequently has seen wild elephants reconnoitre dangerous ground by means of a scout or spy; communicate intelligence by signs; retreat in orderly silence from a lurking danger, and systematically march, in single file, like the jungle tribes of men.

William T. Hornaday, *The Minds and Manners of Wild Animals: A Book of Personal Observations*, New York: Scribner, 1922

They instinctively avoid bad food: thus they do not enter a tract of land in India, named Phalacra, where eating the grass leads to loss of hair and tusks.

Aelian, *De Natura Animalium*, VIII, 15

No jungle wallah and no Burmans would ever camp near *lwins* [small open marshes in dense jungle: breeding grounds for malarial mosquitoes], and . . . as for elephants, they avoided them like the plague.

J. H. Williams, *Elephant Bill*, London: Rupert Hart-Davis, 1950

Elephants have a perfectly uncanny skill in detecting anything that has been tampered with, as many carnival men have learned when they have tried to poison elephants that had been condemned to death. In one case a creature ate every bag of peanuts out of the trolley from which she was accustomed to steal such delicacies every day, except the few that contained the tasteless and odourless poison planted therein to kill her. These she hurled aside with rage and contempt. There is usually an abundance of food in the jungles, so that elephants have no cause to test, let alone eat, morsels that have been handled by men whose smell they abhor.

Ivan T. Sanderson, *The Dynasty of Abu: A History and Natural History of the Elephants and Their Relatives Past and Present*, London: Cassell, 1960

When on the move, elephants rely to a considerable extent on their sense of smell. They generally run into the wind so that they can detect the enemy far ahead and, if necessary, take evasive action. If they are alarmed while feeding they will raise their trunks above the high grass and sniff the air, like so many submarines pushing up their periscopes to allow the look-out to sweep the horizon . . . They can pick up every scent from every point of the compass. So keen is their sense of smell that without turning the head, without even looking, they will infallibly avoid a python curled up in the long grass or a wild animal lying hidden anywhere near their path. I have known a nervous herd scent a man at a distance of more than a mile.

William Bazé, *Just Elephants*, translated from the French by H. M. Burton, London: Elek Books, 1955

There are various methods of killing them. Pitfalls are the most common, but the old bulls are seldom caught in this manner . . . The position chosen for the pit is, almost without exception, in the vicinity of a drinking-place . . . The old bulls never approach a watering-place rapidly, but carefully listen for danger, and then slowly advance with their warning trunks stretched to the path before them; the delicate nerves of the proboscis at once detect the hidden snare.

Ivan T. Sanderson, *The Dynasty of Abu: A History and Natural History of the Elephants and Their Relatives Past and Present*, London: Cassell, 1960

Elephants can be absolutely quiet when they want to be – as quiet as stones, in fact – and they sometimes combine this gift with a sort of mimicry. South Annam is strewn with large black rocks, and an elephant who is anxious not to be seen can 'disguise' himself perfectly as one of these rocks; I have often found myself within a few feet of one without having spotted him.

William Bazé, *Just Elephants*, translated from the French by H. M. Burton, London: Elek Books, 1955

The bulkiest elephant moves through the jungle with astonishingly little noise, and is a master of the art of concealment. I remember once trying to photograph a magnificent bull on the Kenya–Tanganyika border. My companion and I were on foot, and the elephant was approaching us along the further side of a row of bushes. We hurried, as we thought, unobserved, to the end of the row, where we waited for him to appear. There was complete silence, and as within half a minute he was not visible, we peered round the last bush, half expecting to meet him face to face. Instead, although the cover was by no means dense, we found he had completely disappeared. We followed in the only direction he could have taken, but never saw him again. He had become aware of our presence and vanished as softly and silently as a ghost.

Richard Carrington, *Elephants*, London: Chatto & Windus, 1958

I took much curious delight in watching his [the elephant's] antics – yea, in striving to converse with him, for the understanding of these creatures is wonderfully lively.

Michel de Montaigne, *Essays*, trans. Charles Cotton, London: T. Basset, 1693

The brain of the adult African elephant is the heaviest and largest of any living or extinct terrestrial mammal . . . A close examination of the elephant brain, however, combined with actual experience of living elephants in the wild and in captivity, yields abundant evidence that the elephant both possesses the mechanism and demonstrates the capacity for intelligence . . .

The cerebellum is remarkably similar to man in having the anterior lobe . . . One additional trait of the elephant is present among the larger cetaceans. Each lobule is extensively subdivided into folia or folds. In proportion to size the lobules decidedly exceed those in number of the human cerebellum. Although the functional significance of the trait remains unknown it is characteristic of all orders usually considered to rank among the most specialised of mammals.

Sylvia K. Sikes, *The Natural History of the African Elephant*, London: Weidenfeld & Nicolson, 1971

Certainly, there is something special about the elephant – not just its size, or its long life, or its ivory; there is something else, perhaps its intelligence, that somehow sets it apart from other African animals.

Cynthia Moss, 'The Amboseli Elephants', *Wildlife News*, 12: 2, 9–12, 1977

Towards the end of the fourth day the herd came to a stream . . . It was not easy for them to drink because the stream was so shallow. It followed the flat bottom of a valley before running between two high rocks and forming a waterfall a short distance away. The thirsty elephants stirred up mud with their feet and bumped one against the other. Many of them trumpeted to show their irritation.

A few, meanwhile, have moved downstream towards the waterfall. Some sucked up the rushing water for their own pleasure, but others did something quite unexpected. They threw branches and stones across the narrowing river bed; they even tore up whole bushes and trees from the banks and piled them up, helter-skelter, their roots still dripping with dirt. This disorderly heap began to form a plug at the top of the waterfall. Soon the water was effectively dammed and its level rose perceptibly.

Elephants can build dams. A number of hunters claim to have seen them at work; the details of their accounts seem trustworthy and they have been checked against each other. Elephants' dams are not nearly so impressive, in comparison to their relative size, as beavers'; neither are they anywhere nearly as ingeniously planned and constructed. But the beaver has been from time immemorial an architect, and spent much of his life in dam-building. In him this activity is almost instinctive, although according to the latest trend of animal psychology, instinct and intelligence are not clearly differentiated. Elephants, on the other hand, rarely build dams, and then only under the pressure of necessity. The idea that a dam raises the level of the water behind it is not ever-present in their minds; it comes to the fore only in certain topographical circumstances. Unlike bees, they are not all equally skilled workers, and this is evidence of intelligence rather than instinctual behaviour. 'In the wilds of Africa,' writes Albert Jeannin [A. Jeannin, *L'elephant d'Afrique: zoologie, histoire, chasse, protection*, Paris, 1947], 'elephants perform deliberate acts, which can arise only out of a logical train of thought.'

When the dam was finished the water was four feet deeper than before. The elephants were able to drink and bathe to their heart's content, to pump up the water noisily and shower one another. They stayed all night beside this improvised reservoir.

Georges Blond, *The Elephants*, translated from the French by Frances Frenaye, London: Andre Deutsch, 1962

There are numerous accounts of elephant intelligence in relation to their work in lumber camps in Sri Lanka, India and other Asian countries. Elephants seem to understand the concept of balance and symmetry in loading and stacking timber logs.

Dr Jack Adams, *Wild Elephants in Captivity, Elephant Training Procedures: Step-by-step methods formerly kept secret by trainers throughout the world*, Carson, California: The Center for the Study of Elephants, 1981

One of the elephants [in the forest department at Trivandrum, Kerala] has just piled a huge log neatly on the stack. The mahout relaxes. It has been a difficult job. But the elephant is still on the alert. He walks back, looks at his handiwork from one angle and another, decides it's no good the way it is, steps forward again, and adjusts the log whose alignment had not been perfect.

Another time I saw man and beast approach a big stack with one more huge log to pile on. The man wore a purposeful look on his face. The expression of the elephant, in its own way, was sceptical, hesitant, groping. *Hut hut*, the mahout incited. But it was to no avail. Mallawtee, the elephant, stopped dead in her tracks. *Hut hut*, the man swung his bamboo. 'Don't you see, you fool, that the pile won't hold if we unload another log on it – that the day's work will come crashing down?' This is what Mallawtee seemed to say, and she dropped the log she was carrying. This fetched her a blow from the angry mahout's bamboo cane, which came whistling down on her sensitive trunk . . . Mallawtee answered with a contemptuous snort. Let the little fool yell up there, she seemed to say, he does not have an inkling of engineering finesse. It's too bad. And at that she approached the pile and began to push and pull the logs until they formed an adequate basis on which to build further. Then she went to pick up her log and deposited it safely on top of the others.

The mahout smiled, as if all this had been his own idea in the beginning.

Elisabeth Mann Borgese, *The Language Barrier: Beasts and Men*, New York: Holt, Rinehart & Winston, 1968

To watch an elephant building a bridge, to see the skill with which the great beast lifted the huge logs and the accuracy with which they were coaxed into position, was to realize that the trained elephant was no mere transport animal, but indeed a skilled sapper.

Field-Marshal Sir William Slim, in the foreword to J. H. Williams, *Elephant Bill*, London: Rupert Hart-Davis, 1950

A circus elephant was chained near a hay and grain barn. This elephant was capable of removing the steel bolt in the latch that kept the door to the barn locked. The elephant manipulated the bolt until he worked it out of the latch, dropped it to the ground, pulled open the door to the barn with its trunk, and fed on the grain and hay. This episode occurred on at least three different occasions. Each time that the bolt was removed and the barn door opened by the elephant, a trainer would scold the elephant and close the barn door by replacing the bolt into the latch. The fourth time, the trainer could not find the steel bolt that was usually dropped near the door by the elephant. A lady observer standing nearby informed the trainer that the elephant had been extending its trunk high up to a window ledge that was located above the door. The trainer obtained a ladder, climbed up to the window ledge, and found the bolt that was placed there by the elephant. Was the elephant trying to hide the bolt so that the door to the barn could not be locked by the trainer? The trainer was sure of it, and he claimed that this was the most intelligent behaviour he had ever seen an elephant perform in his more than 35 years of experience.

Dr Jack Adams, *Wild Elephants in Captivity, Elephant Training Procedures: Step-by-step methods formerly kept secret by trainers throughout the world*, Carson, California: The Center for the Study of Elephants, 1981

After elephants have been trained in captivity through negative reinforcement administered by a trainer with his bull-hook, elephants tend to respond appropriately to verbal commands and a simple placement of the bull-hook on their body. So elephants have learned that discretion is the better part of valour. This certainly would be interpreted as intelligent behaviour.

Dr Jack Adams, *Wild Elephants in Captivity, Elephant Training Procedures: Step-by-step methods formerly kept secret by trainers throughout the world*, Carson, California: The Center for the Study of Elephants, 1981

J. H. Williams gives an account of another almost unbelievable incident. A number of young elephants . . . developed the habit of stuffing mud into the wooden bells they wore around their necks so that they could no longer ring. Then they stole bananas during the night. In this way they managed to plunder entire banana groves in the immediate vicinity of the plantation owner's house.

Karl-Erik Fichtelius & Sverre Sjölander, *Man's Place: Intelligence in Whales, Dolphins, and Humans*, London: Gollancz, 1973

M*utiannus* who was thrice Consul affirmed to *Pliny* that he saw an Elephant which learned the Greek letters, and was able with his tongue to write these words: Autos egoo Tadegrapsa laphura tekelt anetheca: that is, I wrote these things and dedicated the Celtic spoils: but in these actions of writing, the hand of the teacher must be also present to teach him how to frame the letters, and then as *Aelianus* says they will write upon Tables, and follow the true proportion of the Characters expressed before their face, whereupon they look as attentively as any *Grammarian*.

Edward Topsell, *The History of Four-Footed Beasts, describing the True and Lively Figure of every Beast . . . collected out of all the Volumes of C. Gesner and all other Writers of the Present Day*, London: W. Jaggard, 1607

The artist was a native of the Far East – specifically the kingdom of Thailand. She was an adolescent member of the endangered species *Elephas maximus*. She was Siri, fourteen years old in 1982, eight feet tall at the shoulder, an 8,400 pound Asian elephant.

Siri did most of the drawings in Gucwa [her keeper]'s presence, though he did not teach her to draw, nor had he ever rewarded her for doing so. She drew only when she wanted to, using a pencil held in the curl of her trunk to sketch on a pad Gucwa held in his lap. Most of the drawings were done on nine-by-twelve inch and fifteen-by-eighteen paper sheets. Siri produced dozens of designs in concrete before she ever laid eyes on pencil and paper, indeed, it was such work that inspired Gucwa to offer the animal drawing tools in the first place. She created the images at night, while quite alone in the zoo, apparently for her own amusement, using a pebble held in her trunk to scratch in the hard floor of her enclosure.

The medium was her own conception. The message was anybody's guess.

David Gucwa & James Ehmann, *To Whom It May Concern: An Investigation of the Art of Elephants*, New York: W. W. Norton, 1985

Once you understand that an animal's intelligent, it's not illogical to suspect that it might be creative.

Now an elephant's trunk is a pathway of emotional energy – it is capable of violence, it is capable of caressing. So it is also not illogical to suspect that, through her trunk, she might channel the same emotional energy into drawing.

David Gucwa, keeper, from David Gucwa & James Ehmann, *To Whom It May Concern: An Investigation of the Art of Elephants*, New York: W. W. Norton, 1985

In Buddhism the elephant remains symbolic as the vehicle for divine teachings, a symbol of divine truth. Traditional Buddhists believe that a person will do very well if he models his character on the elephant's.

With that in mind David Gucwa confronted a curious coincidence when he met Jun Yashuda, a native of Japan and a member of the Nipoponzan Myohooi order of Buddhist nuns. He showed her the picture [below right] before explaining its origins. Jun-san smiled immediately. She bowed to the photo.

'What does it mean?' Gucwa asked.

'It is Buddha,' she said. 'If other Japanese or Chinese people see this picture, I think they say the same answer, because 佛 is the picture's line. It is like a Chinese letter. Japanese people also use the same letter. The letter's meaning: 'Buddha'.

David Gucwa & James Ehmann, *To Whom It May Concern: An Investigation of the Art of Elephants*, New York: W. W. Norton, 1985

So perfect is the control of the motion of the trunk that a young elephant of the forest department at Trivandrum, Kerala, was taught a few years ago to pick up, not a log, but a normal-sized piece of chalk, to walk up to the blackboard and *write* in a firm, legible longtrunk, '*Welcome*.'

Elisabeth Mann Borgese, *The Language Barrier: Beasts and Men*, New York: Holt, Rinehart & Winston, 1968

'All our elephants draw,' McCusker [Steve McCusker, curator of animals, Washington Park Zoo, Portland, Oregon] said. He noted in passing that, while Portland's zoo staffers had all witnessed the behaviour, none of them had ever given it much thought.

David Gucwa & James Ehmann, *To Whom It May Concern: An Investigation of the Art of Elephants*, New York: W. W. Norton, 1985

While it is generally fruitless and unsatisfactory to enter the field of speculation, I cannot resist the temptation to assert my belief that an elephant can be taught to read written characters, and also to express some of his own thoughts or states of feeling in writing. It would be a perfectly simple matter to prepare suitable appliances by which the sagacious animal could hold a crayon in his trunk, and mark upon a surface adapted to his convenience. Many an elephant has been taught to make chalk-marks on a blackboard. In Aelian's work on 'The Nature of Animals', the eleventh chapter of the second book, he describes in detail the wonderful performances of elephants at Rome, all of which he saw. One passage is of peculiar interest to us, and the following has been given as a translation: '. . . I saw them writing letters on Roman tablets with their trunks, neither looking awry nor turning aside.'

I can conceive how an elephant may be taught that certain characters represent certain ideas, and that they are capable of intelligent combinations.

William T. Hornaday, Director of the New York Zoological Park, *The Minds and Manners of Wild Animals: A Book of Personal Observations*, New York: Scribner, 1922

We do know that the elephant can understand our language. That he learns the precise sound and meaning of up to sixty words is quite common and well documented. Perhaps he can learn much more than that. One mahout claimed that his elephant understood *everything* he said, which might even be credible, when you consider that the mahout was a very simple boy whose own vocabulary probably did not exceed a few hundred words.

But we know even more . . . Bernard Rensch [B. Rensch, 'The Intelligence of Elephants', *Scientific American*, 196(2), 44–9, 1957] has demonstrated that an elephant can learn to distinguish as many as twenty-six abstract designs, among them letters of the alphabet and numbers. Not only could he learn these within the course of a very few months, but he could remember them after an interval of four and a half months: so excellent was his memory.

We furthermore know that elephants are able to associate sound with sign. You put a rope and a chain in front of the elephant. You pronounce 'rope' and he will pick it up and give you the rope. If you attach a shield with the word ROPE to the rope, and one with the word CHAIN to the chain, the elephant learns quickly to associate the image of the letters with that of the object and will pick up the shield marked CHAIN upon verbal command, even if there is no longer any chain present.

Taken together, these capacities – the ability to learn a human vocabulary, to distinguish abstract design, and to associate sound and sign – should enable the elephant to learn to read and write, at least in a mechanical way.

Elisabeth Mann Borgese, *The Language Barrier: Beast and Men*, New York: Holt, Rinehart & Winston, 1968

He [the elephant] learns to remember such melodies as can only be remembered by people acquainted with music . . .

Abu al-Fazl ibn Mubarak (called 'Allami'), *Ain i Akbari*, translated from the Persian by H. Blochmann and H. S. Jarrett, Calcutta, 1873

I have myself seen an elephant clanging cymbals, and others dancing; two cymbals were fastened to the player's forelegs, and one on his trunk, and he rhythmically beat with his trunk the cymbal on either leg in turn; the dancers danced in a circle, and raising and bending their forelegs in turn moved rhythmically, as the player with the cymbals marked the time for them.

Megasthenes, an account of India in four books, quoted in Arrian, *Indica*

Keeper Dick Richards [of the New York Zoological Park] easily taught Alice to blow a mouth organ . . . and to turn a hand-organ at the proper speed.

William T. Hornaday, Director of the New York Zoological Park, *The Minds and Manners of Wild Animals: A Book of Personal Observations*, New York: Scribner, 1922

Our observations of the Indian working elephants' ability to learn a vocabulary of verbal commands prompted us to make a precise laboratory examination of our elephant's acoustic discrimination. Our collaborator J. Reinert carried out these experiments. He started with a pair of pure tones: the tone at 750 cycles per second was the positive stimulus and 500 cycles per second (three full notes lower in pitch) was the negative one. The sounds were produced electronically through a loudspeaker. To make the elephant's learning behaviour more easily observable it was taught to 'stand at attention' at the beginning of each series of trials: she had to grasp the lower iron bar of her cage with her trunk. If the sound presented was the 'wrong' one, she was supposed to remain in this position. If it was the right one, she was to knock on the lid of a switch box in front of her cage with her trunk: this caused an electrical gadget to bring a food reward within reach of her trunk. The experimenter sat behind a screen watching the animal by means of a mirror system.

The elephant learned to discriminate six pairs of sounds, one of which differed by only a single full note. In tests on all of them in irregular rotation she was able to distinguish all 12 tones and to know their positive or negative meaning. From these results one may conclude that the elephant possesses an excellent memory of absolute pitch. Again in this case she demonstrated remarkably long retention: after a lapse of a year and a half, during which she went on to other acoustic learning, she was able to get nine out of 12 of the pitch discriminations correct on a return to the test.

In the meantime we had examined the elephant's ability to learn short melodies. The positive sound pattern was a melody consisting of three tones – low, high and low. The negative melody also had three tones, but the pattern was reversed: the second tone was lower than the first and the third higher than the second. After the elephant had fully learned these two melodies, they were altered by all possible means: shifted towards higher or lower frequencies, changed in intensity, rhythm or timing, played on various instruments that varied their timbre. In spite of all these alterations the elephant was able to recognize the positive and negative melodies (i.e. the relations of notes) in the overwhelming majority of the trials.

Bernhard Rensch, 'The Intelligence of Elephants', *Scientific American*, 196(2), 44–9, 1957

The surgeon, Sir Everard Home, who carried out an exhaustive anatomical examination of the elephant's ear, maintained that its structure precluded the animal from having any appreciation of music.

Charles Knight, *The Elephant Principally Viewed in Relation to Man*, London: C. Knight & Co., 1844

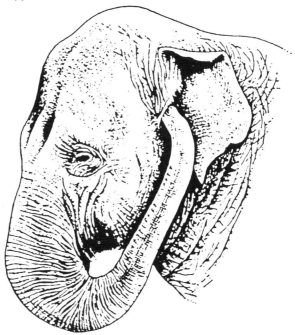

Should the attention of an individual in the herd be attracted by any unusual appearance in the forest, the intelligence is rapidly communicated by a low suppressed sound made by the lips, somewhat resembling the twittering of a bird, and described by the hunters by the word '*prut*'.

Sir J. Emmerson Tennent, *Sketches of the Natural History of Ceylon . . . including a monograph on the Elephant*, London: Longman, Green, Longman & Roberts, 1861

Of elephant language, little has been recorded, nothing has been analysed. We know that elephants emit three types of sound: a hum, a whistle, and a roar. According to the Mudevan tribesmen, the humming sound indicates a warning, and there are several variants of it: 'Tiger approaching', 'Man approaching', 'Fire', and perhaps others. The whistling – still according to the tribesmen – means that one of the herd has been injured or is otherwise in distress. The roar is a threat or signal to attack. These tribesmen probably know more than anybody else about voices in the jungle; on the other hand, their testimony must always be taken with a grain of salt. They like to show off, or at any rate to tell you what they think you want to hear. However this may be, the 'vocabulary' as they explain it sounds quite plausible and does not exceed what we would expect. On the contrary, considering the social habits of the elephant and the differentiation of his actions and reactions, we could well imagine that his 'language' should be more varied and that elephants should be able to communicate with the precision, let's say, of the bees.

Elisabeth Mann Borgese, *The Language Barrier: Beast and Men*, New York: Holt, Rinehart & Winston, 1968

It is said that Elephants talk to one another, mumbling with their mouths the speech of men. But not to all is the speech of the beasts audible, but only the men who tame them hear it.

Oppian, *Cynegetica*, II, 529–55

Ptolemy Philadelphus was presented with a young elephant which understood the Greek language of the district where it had been brought up. Hitherto it was believed that elephants understood only the language spoken by Indians.

Aelian, *De Natura Animalium*, XI, 25

No attempts have been made to teach elephants to vocalize, the way dolphins do. Whether the elephant could learn to pronounce human words, we do not know. If he could, it would probably cost him extreme efforts.

Elisabeth Mann Borgese, *The Language Barrier: Beasts and Men*, New York: Holt, Rinehart & Winston, 1968

```
VNNN
     EPA132
        :RADIO BROADCASTS +INTERVIEW+ WITH BABY ELEPHANT:
    MOSCOW, JULY 13, REUTER - A LOCAL RADIO STATION HAS
BROADCAST AN +INTERVIEW+ WITH A BABY ELEPHANT AT A ZOO IN THE
SOVIET CENTRAL ASIAN REPUBLIC OF KAZAKHSTAN, THE OFFICIAL SOVIET
NEWS AGENCY TASS REPORTED TODAY.
    TASS SAID THE ELEPHANT, NAMED BATIR, SPOKE NEARLY 20 PHRASES
INTO TAPE RECORDERS FOR ZOOLOGISTS.
    IT ADDED THAT THE ZOOLOGISTS WERE CHECKING A CLAIM BY THE
WATCHMAN AT THE ZOO THAT BATIR TALKED DURING THE NIGHT.
    THE AGENCY QUOTED THE ELEPHANT AS SAYING: +BATIR IS GOOD,
BATIR IS A FINE FELLOW.+
    ELEPHANTS ARE NOT ON THE LIST OF ANIMALS CAPABLE OF
IMITATING HUMAN SPEECH. BUT BATIR IS SAID TO HAVE BEEN RAISED BY
HUMANS FROM A VERY EARLY AGE AND HAVE EXCEPTIONAL HEARING.
 REUTER BK/JCK
```

Reuter report, Moscow, 13 July 1983

Karaganda, Kazakhstan. 12-year-old he-elephant Batir of the Karaganda Zoo is capable of imitating human speech. The elephant speaks mainly about himself and his needs: 'Batir is good', 'Batir is a fine fellow', 'Water', 'Have you given water to the elephant?'

TASS, Moscow, 22 July 1983

From all around the circle [of elephants] came a soft *poo-poo-poo-poo-poo*. That was the elephants talking to one another. It was so soft that it was scarcely audible; but I had heard it many times before. There isn't the slightest doubt in my mind that each and every elephant knew exactly where we were squatting at the foot of that tree.

John Taylor, *Pondoro: Last of the Ivory Hunters*, London: Frederick Muller, 1956

Elephants are known to have a varied repertoire of vocalization which consists of trumpets, growls, snorts, squeaks, rumbles and roars. Each of these can be modified in a variety of ways. The sounds are emitted from both the trunk and the mouth. Just what each of the sounds mean has not been ascertained. Nevertheless, it is obvious that the vocalizations do convey information to other elephants although we have not yet deciphered the code.

There have been some written accounts of 'tummy rumblings' which have been allegedly heard emanating from wild elephants. Most recent investigations of these alleged noises revealed them to be a form of purring sound, which apparently is not related to the digestive system. When wild elephants are out of sight of each other while browsing in the bush, they keep in communication by the purring sound. In case of approaching danger to any elephant in the herd, the purring stops and the sudden silence alerts the members of the herd. This purring sound has been reported among elephants in captivity.

Dr Jack Adams, *Wild Elephants in Captivity*, *Elephant Training Procedures: Step-by-step methods formerly kept secret by trainers throughout the world*, Carson, California: The Center for the Study of Elephants, 1981

Among the land mammals, the only brains larger than those of man are in the elephants. As Georg von Bekesy has shown, the cochlea in the ear of the elephant is designed for the detection of frequencies lower than those used in human speech. The elephants apparently communicate in regions subsonic for humans. They can also hear the speech frequencies of humans. This apparently is a region for fertile scientific investigation . . . Insofar as this author knows, no research has been done on intraspecies subsonic communication among elephants.

The elephant's large ears presumably have a pinna transform for the subsonic frequencies they use in their communication over long distances. Their long trunk also resonates in these subsonic regions for the production of the low-frequency sounds.

John Lilly, *Communication Between Man and Dolphin: The Possibilities of Talking with Other Species*, New York: Crown, 1978

Calls at frequencies below the range of human hearing (14 to 24 hz) were recorded from two groups of captive Asian elephants . . . Elephants are the first terrestrial mammals reported to produce infrasound. These calls may be important in the coordination of behaviour in thick vegetation or among separated groups of elephants.

Katherine B. Payne, William R. Langbauer Jr, & Elizabeth M. Thomas, 'Infrasonic calls of the Asian Elephant (*Elephas maximus*)', *Behavioral Ecology and Sociobiology*, 18(4), 297–301, 1986

Cornell University researchers have recorded low-frequency calls emitted from an elephant's forehead, where the skin over an opening to the nasal passages vibrates like a drum. They suspect that the sound actually begins in the vocal cords. It is so low that it normally escapes human ears.

Low-frequency sounds can travel for more than 12 miles. If this is one way elephants 'speak' . . . it would explain the giant animals' complex social behaviour . . .

The only other example of low-frequency communication among mammals is the call of another highly social creature, the whale.

'Elephant Talk', New York: *Science Digest*, June 1986

Biologist Katharine B. Payne of Cornell University discovered the inaudible sounds by accident while standing near a group of Asian elephants at a zoo in Portland, Oregon. She felt a strange discomfort, she recalls, almost like the rumbling of distant thunder. Flying home, she theorized that the elephants had been calling to one another infrasonically, much like the fin and blue whales are known to do.

Payne enlisted her colleagues William R. Langbauer Jr, Elizabeth M. Thomas and Joyce Poole, and they set off with tape recorders to various captive and wild elephant habitats, including Kenya's Amboseli Park. By speeding up the playback of the recordings they were able to hear a series of calls lasting five to ten seconds each for up to ten minutes at a time – intense calls that could travel several miles through trees, shrubs and tall grass.

If the researchers have indeed uncovered infrasonic communication among elephants, it could explain much about the animals' behaviour, such as the way elephant groups miles apart from one another mysteriously mobilize and unite to face danger.

Dava Sobel, 'Infrasonic Elephants', New York: *Omni*, September 1986

The sounds are at frequencies in the range well below the threshold of human hearing.

It is the first evidence that land mammals can produce infrasonic sounds, and it adds the elephants' basso calls to the wildlife choir that includes the high-frequency shrieks of bats, the soprano voices of porpoises, the alto wails of wolves and coyotes and the tenor-to-bass-range songs of humpback whales. The significance and role of such sounds, audible to people or not, has long puzzled wildlife biologists.

'This discovery is like suddenly finding a tribe with a hitherto unknown language,' said Dr Thomas Lovejoy, vice president for science of the World Wildlife Fund in Washington. 'I think it will add a whole new dimension to our understanding of elephant communications and social systems.'

Such a communications system would be an asset to a society whose families are divided into groups with different degrees of stability, different schedules and different reasons for gathering or dispersion, Payne said. Observers of both Asian and African elephants have been puzzled for years by occurrences of sudden coordinated movements of large groups of elephants when no signal was apparent to human observers. 'The use of infrasonic calls may offer an explanation for this,' Payne said.

Bayard Webster, 'Elephants Can Call Long Distance', *New York Times*, reprinted in *This World*, 23 March 1986

If we are to compare the basic elements of human social life with those of any other species, we need to use analogies, because many of the functions these elements serve simply are not served in any other primate species. Primates do not have big cooperative enterprises, nor therefore the loyalty, fidelity, and

developed skills that go with them. Nor do they have fixed homes and families. But the hunting carnivores do. And neither apes nor wolves have anything like the human length of life, nor therefore the same chance of accumulating wisdom and of deepening relationships. But elephants do . . . This is why it is vacuous to talk of 'the difference between man and animal' without saying *which* animal.

Several groups of animals, *not* closely related, have independently 'invented' fairly advanced forms of social life. They are, that is, not 'anonymous herds' whose members stay together but take no notice of one another. They can *do* things together, help and look after one another to some extent, and have individual friendships. Examples are (at their own level) many birds (such as geese and jackdaws), such carnivores as wolves and wild dogs, elephants, many primates, and probably whales and dolphins . . .

Right across this range, social life shows certain common structural features. The first of these, noted by Lorenz, can be crudely summed up by saying that *it rests on peacemaking* – that the positive social bond consists of friendly gestures that arise from the need to counter an existing possibility of aggression. Species incapable of mutual attack do not, apparently, ever find the occasion to become friends . . .

If one asks, what holds this bunch of creatures together? the answer is attachment: a bond of affection constantly fed and maintained by friendly attention. It is not fear. Many of these creatures can survive on their own very well, and sometimes do so when they feel like being solitary. (Elephants and gorillas are impressive examples.) It is not food. Only the hunting carnivores tap the economic advantage of cooperating. They just like each other. And not indiscriminately; they have preferences.

Mary Midgley, *Beast & Man: The Roots of Human Nature*, Brighton: Harvester, 1979

The herd will include parents and children, brothers and sisters, uncles, aunts, nephews, nieces, and possibly a sprinkling of in-laws who have been accepted into the group from outside. The number of individuals will vary considerably, ranging from ten to twelve in a small herd to fifty or more in a large one. Some herds are even larger than this, and I have seen vast assemblages of African elephants on the Nile and in Tanganyika between one and two hundred strong. These exceptionally large herds are not composed of members of the same family, but are temporary associations of smaller herds brought together in one place by seasonal shortages of water and pasturage. While the shortage lasts, the smaller herds will remain together in the region of the supply, but as conditions improve they will split up once more into their original family groups. During the period of association they constantly intermingle, and it is possible that a certain interchange of individuals may take place before the family herds fan out into their former habitats. New social units may also be formed at these times, as a result of two animals from different herds going off on one of the elephantine honeymoons . . . and thus forming the nucleus of a herd of their own.

Richard Carrington, *Elephants*, London: Chatto & Windus, 1958

Elephants vary in temperament and disposition in much the same way as human beings. Every individual is different and it is unwise to make up one's mind about them, collectively or singly, until one has lived with them a long time and got to know them intimately.

William Bazé, *Just Elephants*, translated from the French by H. M. Burton, London: Elek Books, 1955

Each herd has an acknowledged leader, and most naturalists agree that this is usually a female. At first the idea of a female leader may seem rather unusual, but we should remember that a matriarchal organization is also found among other kinds of animals and in many human races . . . The bull elephant is not without his uses, however. His size alone is expressive of physical power, and his superior armament in the form of larger tusks enables him to present a bold front to the world in case of danger. He is, in fact, both virile and handsome, and it would be rash to assume that these qualities do not excite the same emotional reactions among the female of the species in the elephant world as they do in the world of men. On occasion, also, bulls can exhibit a comforting tenderness, and numerous writers have remarked on the touching attentions they pay to their mates during the period of the honeymoon.

Richard Carrington, *Elephants*, London: Chatto & Windus, 1958

There was a superabundance of food and after six months on a high quality diet the elephants were fat, healthy, and, to use a word that does not seem very elephantine, frisky. The elephants were behaving in entirely new ways and it was a joy to be with them. Each day I went out I would see fat, happy elephants, doing amazingly silly things. I came to call their general play behaviour 'being silly' because it seemed to be as accurate a term as any . . . It became like a three-ring circus and I could only write down some of what I saw:
—The ones that are playing are using the vegetation a lot, throwing bits about, running through it . . .

—What is interesting is all the adult females playing. There are just as many if not more young females being silly as anyone else. One female has a whole small tree she's tossing around.

—Virginia turns towards Lexi, practically kneels, then sprays moisture from her nose at him.

—Calandre is one of the silliest of all. She charges a minibus by crashing through the bushes.

—They are expending an incredible amount of energy.

—Even Grace is playing now. It's an amazing sight. Grace comes racing out, frightens herself when she almost runs into me, *really trumpets* and scares everyone into running off. Gloria and Gladys and others ran towards her when she trumpeted, then they go tearing off running and play trumpeting all across the open stretch to the arm of the swamp.

Cynthia Moss, *Elephant Memories: Thirteen Years in the Life of an Elephant Family*, London: Elm Tree Books, 1988

In spite of their size elephants are never clumsy. If a herd is alarmed the calves disappear under their mothers, and should a stampede occur it is astonishing that they are not trampled and injured. Yet the known cases of a calf being injured in the most violent stampedes are so few as to be negligible.

Richard Carrington, *Elephants*, London: Chatto & Windus, 1958

The elephant, although a gross beast, is yet the most decent and most sensible of any other upon earth. Although he never changes his female, and hath so tender a love for her whom he hath chosen, yet he never couples with her but at the end of every three years, and then only for the space of five days.

St Francis de Sales, *An Introduction to a Devout Life*, 39, Douai: Iohn Heigham, 1613

Of all the animals in creation the female elephant must be easily the most chaste. Once she has chosen her partner she will refuse the advances of all others, and not until well after her baby is born will she accept the advances of another suitor. By that time her fidelity will have lasted throughout the whole period of gestation and for some months afterwards – in all, an average of three years – so who shall blame her if she begins to look around for a new mate?

William Bazé, *Just Elephants*, translated from the French by H. M. Burton, London: Elek Books, 1955

It was rather like watching from a cliff the movement of yachts in the distance. They drew closer and closer. Then suddenly, when they were within a stone's throw of one another, the silence was broken by a chirp, made by placing the tongue between the teeth against the side of the cheek and then sucking air in, rather like the gee-up sound for a horse. The noise will carry a mile and is a signal of contentment and joy . . . it was as if Bandoola was calling . . . 'Come here. There's a luscious patch of green *kaing* [grass] where I am.' Elephant courtship is tactful, slow and certain. One of the females chirped back. Then guttural rumblings came from Bandoola like the noise of a Rolls-Bentley.

J. H. Williams, *Bandoola*, London: Rupert Hart-Davis, 1953

Well concealed in the bush and perched high enough to be beyond the range of their keen sense of smell, I have several times watched elephants at their amorous antics, and I hereby certify that they have discovered no new tricks; they do just what all other quadrupeds do. But where other animals appear to rush the whole thing, elephants are more sentimental, more tender. They use their trunks to caress each other and to seal their affection. The

female usually holds hers above her head, pointing backwards, and the male grasps the end of it with his own, but this little embrace can equally well take place side-by-side if the lovers prefer holding hands that way.

During the honeymoon the male is full of little attentions for his bride, accompanying her with little kindnesses and whispering a thousand sweet nothings in her ear – although 'whispering' is, perhaps, not quite the appropriate word.

I have never been able to fix the average length of the courtship. According to my notes, the most uxorious . . . continued his amours for three whole months. He seemed to prefer the dark, and it was often during the night that his passion got the better of him . . .

The Moi [of Indo-China] believe . . . that the length of the courtship depends on the temperaments of the partners and their ability to establish complete mutual understanding.

William Bazé, *Just Elephants*, translated from the French by H. M. Burton, London: Elek Books, 1955

They are modest and shamefast about procreation, for at that time they seek woods and secret places, and sometimes the waters because water supports the male in that action, whereby he ascends and descends from the back of the female with more ease. When elephants go to copulation, they turn their heads toward the East, but whether this is done in remembrance of Paradise, or for any other reason, I cannot tell.

Edward Topsell, *The History of Four-Footed Beasts, describing the True and Lively Figure of every Beast . . . collected out of all the Volumes of C. Gesner and all other Writers of the Present Day*, London: W. Jaggard, 1607

The love-making of elephants as I have seen it seems to me more simple and more lovely than any myth. It is beautiful because it is quite without the brutishness and the cruelty which one sees in the mating of so many animals.

Without there being any appearance of season, two animals become attracted by each other. In other words they fall in love, and days, even weeks, of courtship may take place, the male mounting the female with ease and grace and remaining in that position for three or four minutes. Eventually the mating is consummated, and the act lasts five or ten minutes, and may be repeated three or four times during the twenty-four hours. The pair will keep together as they graze for months, and their honeymoon will last all that time. When they have knocked off from the day's work [in the teak plantation] they will call each other and go off together into the jungle. My own belief is that it lasts until the female has been pregnant for ten months – that is, until she has become aware that she is pregnant . . .

J. H. Williams, *Elephant Bill*, London: Rupert Hart-Davis, 1950

Sanderson [G. P. Sanderson, *Thirteen Years Among the Wild Beasts of India*, London: W. H. Allen, 1882] states that female elephants usually give birth to their first calf at 16 years of age and continue to breed till they reach the age of 80.

G. H. Evans, *Elephants and Their Diseases: A Treatise on Elephants*, Rangoon, Burma: Government Printing, 1910

The cows are remarkably good with their young. They will fondle them affectionately with their trunks, wash them, and keep a constant eye on them to see that they do not stray into danger; they also impose a rigid discipline and spank them severely whenever their youthful high spirits cause them to be insubordinate. But such severity is based on genuine maternal affection and, moreover, extends to calves other than the mother's own. It is an appealing trait in elephants that, if a calf is orphaned, it will always find another cow in the herd who will accept it as her foster-child.

Richard Carrington, *Elephants*, London: Chatto & Windus, 1958

In a wild state, the baby elephants are the pets of the entire herd and both cows and bulls shower affection on them. The grown up elephants allow the babies to take any liberties and show them great patience and toleration.

An authority on Indian elephants tells of our elephants . . . which gave birth to young about the same time. The first cow's calf was born in September, another in October, a third in February and the fourth in March. These four young elephants would go to any cow and they would suckle them and mother them as though they were their own. Often two of the youngsters were seen nursing the same cow, each sucking one of her teats.

Edmund Heller, 'Elephants, In and Out of the Zoo', *Bulletin of the Washington Park Zoological Society of Milwaukee*, May 1933

Play begins at an early age and may, at least in males, persist into adulthood. Calves of all ages form constantly changing play groups that include members of different families. They push, roll, gambol, and use their trunks to slap and wrestle . . . when partners of uneven sizes play, the stronger matches its strength to that of the weaker. Mothers or adolescent females may intervene in playfights in support of young calves if the calf is knocked down by a larger playmate or if the play becomes too rough and threatens to escalate. A young calf's earliest play consists of solo charges and rushes. These locomotor routines occur within the safe circle of the calf's family, but they may also extend the calf's range to nearby areas, exposing the calf to accidental injury or to predation. In such cases older female members of the calf's family seem to respond quickly to the danger.

Robert Fagen, *Animal Play Behaviour*, Oxford: Oxford University Press, 1981

Unable to cross a ditch, the largest one drops into the gap and acts as a bridge; when the rest have crossed over on his back, they rescue him before moving on: this is done by one on the bank thrusting his foot forward for the trapped elephant to grasp with his trunk, while others throw undergrowth into the ditch.

Aelian, *De Natura Animalium*, VIII, 15

Most hunters assert that elephants help their wounded and that two or three of them will raise a fallen comrade and then take him away by holding him up on each side and by pushing from behind. Other 'experts' deny this and seem quite certain that elephants never aid one that has fallen into a pit. Sanderson [G. P. Sanderson, *Thirteen Years Among the Wild Beasts of India*, London: W. H. Allen, 1882], however, states that he knew cases of herd bulls coming miles to unshackle a captured colleague and of one that built a ramp with logs in a pit and hauled out a cow. Several people have related that elephants bogged in mud or quicksand will save themselves, if planks are thrown to them, at first making a catwalk, climbing on to this, and then taking the boards one at a time from behind and placing them in front, and so moving on to safety.

There is the famous case of Jim Brown, the director of the Fort Worth Zoo in Texas, who was saved from certain death under the feet of one elephant by another – the famous old Queen Tut, *doyenne* of that zoo; there is Bill Williams's now almost immortal Bandoola, who led the last refugees out of

Burma over the precipitous Naga Hills just ahead of the Japanese invaders in World War II; and there are many other such cases. Their actions sometimes seem to demonstrate mental processes of the very highest order.

Recognizing that a creature of another species is in danger from one's own kind; going to the aid of that creature; fighting off its molesters; picking it up and carrying it to safety, and all without any command, are acts of cerebration, and they imply the exercise of true compassion and also some other most sensitive emotions. A dog can be trained to defend his master against other dogs, but in the above instance Queen Tut was *not* trained to do anything. She was a zoo exhibit: Jim Brown was a zoo director.

Ivan T. Sanderson, *The Dynasty of Abu: A History and Natural History of the Elephants and Their Relatives Past and Present*, London: Cassell, 1960

The fine tusker, Chandrasekharan, belonging to HH The Maharaja of Travancore, died last year of old age.

The elephant was particularly remarkable for his sagacity, gentleness and almost human intelligence. He never harmed a living creature till his death. Various stories are current evidencing one or other of his qualities, an authentic one being his refusal to erect a pillar in one of the pits dug for the purpose in connection with one of the Murajapan festivals in Trivandrum. Usually the elephant was a very willing worker and his refusal to hoist the pillar which he held still with his tusk and trunk surprised the mahout who on looking into the pit found that a dog which had strayed in had got into the pit and fallen asleep. It was only after the dog was roused and driven away that Chandrasekharan lowered the pillar into the pit.

N. G. Pillai, Curator of the State Museum at Trivandrum, 22 August 1941, 'On the Height and Age of an Elephant', *Journal of the Bombay Natural History Society*, 42: 4, 927–8, 1941

Not every unlikely story concerning elephants can be dismissed as idle superstition. For example, the tradition that they will help one another in difficulties, and that the herd is loth to desert one of its members who is injured or wounded, is well substantiated. Commander Blunt tells how he was called one evening to an African village where elephants had been continually raiding. He went at once in search of the miscreants and soon came across a party of four bulls. He fired at the brain of one of them and missed, but the elephant nevertheless went down. Blunt continues:

'Immediately the three others closed in on him, one on either side and one behind, and they just boosted him on to his feet and, in that formation, supporting him on either side, set off, wheeling gradually round to the left and back to the forest. That was the first time I had seen such a thing, and I stood amazed.'

Richard Carrington, *Elephants*, London: Chatto & Windus, 1958

Even in captivity, the animals show concern for one another. Eventually the St Louis zoo's dancing elephant, Honey, got too sick to perform in the zoo's daily show. She had an infection in her feet, and, as it later turned out, cancer of the lungs. When the day came that Honey couldn't get up to perform, the show had to be called off: the other four elephants wouldn't leave her. Since her illness was incurable, she was put to death.

George W. 'Slim' Lewis, *Elephant Tramp*, London: Peter Davies, 1955

Harvey Croze [the Elephant Warden of the Serengeti] and a photographer friend of his witnessed the death of an old cow in the middle of her family unit in the Serengeti. Her dying dragged out over an afternoon in that lovely rolling northern country . . . Harvey first noticed her lagging behind the family unit: when she fell they all clustered around her, putting their trunks in her mouth, pushing against her and trying to raise her. The most prominent was an independent bull who happened to be with the cows and calves, and he at times kept the others at bay while he attempted alone to aid the dying elephant. She died there among her family, and they stayed with her for several hours longer. The bull in his frustration at failing to raise her . . . mounted the dead cow as if he were attempting to copulate, before finally moving off with the others. One cow, presumably she had a particularly strong bond with the dead animal, stayed longer than the others, only withdrawing reluctantly at nightfall.

Iain & Oria Douglas-Hamilton, *Among the Elephants*, London: Collins & Harvill Press, 1975

Several examples of maternal devotion have been recorded, of which the most striking is perhaps that quoted by Williams in *Elephant Bill*. He tells how one of his working elephants named Ma Shwe (or Miss Gold) was trapped in the flooded Taungdwin River in Burma with her three-month-old calf. The calf was screaming with terror and bobbing about in the water like a cork. It was in constant danger of being swept away, but by tremendous efforts the mother kept hooking it back with her trunk and pressing it against the side of her body. Eventually a sudden rise in the water tore the calf from her side and swept it downstream. Although the river was now a raging torrent, the mother plunged after it and with great difficulty managed to catch it again. She pinned it with her head and trunk against the bank, and then, by a tremendous feat of strength, lifted it completely clear of the water with her trunk and deposited it in safety on a rocky ledge some five feet above flood level. A second later she herself was swept away, and Williams thought she would probably be dashed to pieces in a gorge some three hundred yards downstream. However, she managed to escape, and came hurrying back to where she had left her baby, at first roaring anxiously, and then rumbling with pleasure to see the calf still safe. But unfortunately she had got out of the river on the opposite bank, and the two animals were separated by the torrent. Night was falling and there was nothing that could be done to help. Williams went down several times during the evening and found the calf still on its ledge; but the beam of his torch seemed to disturb the animal, so he decided to leave it in peace till morning. At first light he was relieved to find that the flood level had fallen and Ma Shwe and her baby were reunited. As the river subsided she had obviously plunged into the water once more and lifted down the calf from the ledge in the same way as she had put it there.

This story of courage and altruism is typical of the character of the elephant. Nor can the animal's behaviour be entirely explained as an expression of biological instinct. By deserting her calf in the early stages of the drama she could have saved her own life without difficulty, and thus survived to produce many more members of her species. Instead she preferred to risk death in what must have been a terrifying ordeal with the slight hope of saving the offspring she loved.

Richard Carrington, *Elephants*, London: Chatto & Windus, 1958

Altruism is a behavioural pattern often associated with elephants. Whether or not a particular behaviour can be interpreted as a maternal or sisterly instinct, a self interest, perpetuation of the species or altruism, no one really knows.

Jeheskel Shoshani, 'General Information on Elephants with Emphasis on Tusks', *Elephant* (the publication of the Elephant Interest Group) 2, Detroit: Wayne State University, Department of Biological Sciences, Spring 1976

Some say that the elephant lives for two hundred years; others, for one hundred and twenty.

Aristotle, *Historia Animalium*, IX, 46, 630^b 23

There could be fifty-six (or fourteen sets of) grinding teeth available to the elephant; the first seven sets used up in reaching maturity would really be the milk teeth, and the second seven the permanent adult teeth. This would give the animal its last new set when it was about 120 years old.

Ivan T. Sanderson, *The Dynasty of Abu: A History and Natural History of the Elephants and Their Relatives Past and Present*, London: Cassell, 1960

It was claimed that when Napoleon was in Egypt in 1798–9 he had been given by a Turkish Pasha a live elephant which he had brought back with him to Paris. He had presented the animal [an Indian bull elephant, known as 'Siam'] to his father-in-law Francis, Emperor of Austria (1768–1835), who had deposited it in the Imperial menagerie at Schönbrunn, Vienna. Here it had turned savage, and was passed onto Budapest, where, becoming docile with age, it was still alleged to be living in 1930, aged about 150 years.

Richard Carrington, *Elephants*, London: Chatto & Windus, 1958

In connection with the longevity of animals, concerning which some correspondence appeared in *The Times* a few weeks ago, my attention has been drawn by Dr. P. E. Peiris, Trade Commissioner for Ceylon, to a record of a remarkably long-lived Asiatic elephant. In a translation of Joao Ribeiro's 'Ceilao' by Dr. Peiris (third edition, 1925) mention is made of a famous elephant, Ortela by name, which was probably a fully adult animal prior to the siege of Colombo in 1656, since we are told that the animal at this time had 'offspring and descendants'. The same specimen is referred to by Emerson Tennent in his 'Natural History of Ceylon' (1861) as still being alive when the British flag was hoisted in Colombo in 1796. This elephant is reported by Tennent to have been found in the stables by the Dutch on the expulsion of the Portuguese in 1656 and served under them during the entire period of their occupation, more than 140 years. During the siege of Colombo, Ortela was the only elephant out of 15 animals which was not eaten by the defenders, and it is said that it did much useful work in bringing up trees to repair the breaches in the city walls . . . under the most advantageous circumstances an elephant living for 170 years or so is a fact which is very astonishing.

Guy Dollman, *Journal of the Bombay Natural History Society*, XXXIX, 619, 1937

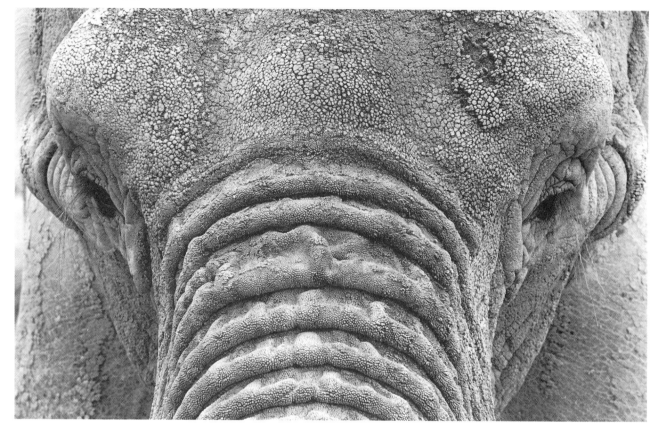

Nowadays, because of the pressures of hunting and poaching, very few elephants die of old age.

John Hanks, *A Struggle for Survival: The Elephant Problem*, London: Country Life Books, 1979

An elephant will not pass by a dead elephant without casting a branch or some dust on the body.

Aelian, *De Natura Animalium*, V, 49

I cannot omit their care, to bury and cover the dead carcasses of their companions, or any others of their kind; for finding them dead they pass not by them till they have lamented their common misery, by casting dust and earth on them, and also green boughs, in token of sacrifice, holding it execrable to do otherwise . . .

Edward Topsell, *The History of Four-Footed Beasts, describing the True and Lively Figure of every Beast . . . collected out of all the Volumes of C. Gesner and all other Writers of the Present Day*, London: W. Jaggard, 1607

Mysterious elephant behaviours have been observed in recent years – behaviours for which no scientific rationale has ever been given. Some of these puzzling incidents include the fact that elephants often bury dead animals, including dead elephant, or parts of them.

Jeheskel Shoshani, 'General Information on Elephants with Emphasis on Tusks', *Elephant* (the publication of the Elephant Interest Group) 2, Detroit: Wayne State University, Department of Biological Sciences, Spring 1976

In a case where an animal is mortally wounded and cannot rise, the other members of the herd circle it disconsolately several times, and if it is still motionless they come to an uncertain halt. They then face outward, their trunks hanging limply to the ground. After a while they may prod and circle again, and then again stand, facing outward. Eventually, if the fallen animal is dead, they move aside and just hang around for several hours, or until nightfall, when they may tear out branches and grass clumps from the surrounding vegetation and drop these on and around the carcass, the younger elephants also taking part in this behaviour. They also scrape soil toward the carcass and then stand by, weaving restlessly from side to side. Eventually they move away from the area.

Sylvia K. Sikes, *The Natural History of the African Elephant*, London: Weidenfeld & Nicolson, 1970

Accounts of elephants burying their own kind are well authenticated. Myles Turner once made a living by taking out hunting parties. On one safari a client shot a large bull elephant out of a herd of about six. The survivors immediately surrounded the dead animal, and stood over him. Myles told his client that the elephants would disperse after a few hours; meanwhile they could retire a little and have their lunch. When they came back some hours later one bull was still by the corpse. The hunters managed to scare it away. Then they advanced to the dead beast and found to their amazement that the other elephants had covered the large wound in its head with mud, and had piled earth and leaves on the body. A similar observation, this time of cows and calves, was made by Irven Buss [I. O. Buss, 'Some observations of food habits and behaviour of the African elephant', *Journal of Wildlife Management*, 25, 131–48, 1961], one of the first scientists to study the elephant's ecology. In Uganda, he had planned to immobilize an elephant and fix a radio on it. The first animal he darted was a cow and he gave it an overdose. The other members of the group closed up in a defensive phalanx with the result that he was unable to administer any antidote and presently the cow died. The leading matriarch took the group away, but returned to cover the cow with branches and grass.

Lastly I must include the experience of the ethologist Wolfdietrich Kühme who made some observations on three captive elephants at the Kronenburg Zoo in Germany [W. Kühme, 'Ethology of the African Elephant', *International Zoo Yearbook*, 4, 113–21, 1963]. The bull when it became aggressive used to throw straw and objects at him over the railings which restricted it. Once Kühme lay down just out of its reach on the far side of the railings. The bull threw straw at him until he was almost completely covered.

Iain & Oria Douglas-Hamilton, *Among the Elephants*, London: Collins & Harvill Press, 1975

They themselves know that the only thing in them that makes desirable plunder is in their weapons which Juba calls 'horns', but which the author so greatly his senior, Herodotus, and also common usage, better term 'teeth' . . .

The tusk alone is ivory . . . The beasts take the greatest care of them; they spare the point of one so that it may not be blunt for fighting and use the other as an implement for digging roots and thrusting massive objects forward; and when surrounded by a party of hunters they post those with the smallest tusks in front, so that it may be thought not worth while to fight them, and afterwards when exhausted they break their tusks by dashing them against a tree and ransom themselves at the price of the desired booty.

Pliny the Elder, *Natural History*, VIII, 7

Many uncanny tales are told concerning elephants and death that even scientists cannot explain. Elephants often bury the dead, including dead elephants, other dead animals they find, and even dead humans they have killed. They cover the bodies with earth and vegetation. A group of scientists and park officials working on a cropping scheme in Uganda collected the ears and feet of the dead elephants to sell later for making handbags and umbrella stands, and put them in a shed. One night a group of elephants broke into the shed and buried the ears and feet. The people involved still feel uncomfortable about the incident.

Another strange and unexplained thing that elephants do is to fondle and examine the bones and tusks of a dead elephant. They often carry bones and tusks away, sometimes a mile or more from the rest of the carcass. This happens frequently in Tsavo, where there is heavy poaching by tribesmen using poison arrows. The elephants are shot and left to die; the hunters come back a few days later to pull the tusks from the already rotting carcasses. It has seriously been considered that the elephants know their companions are being killed for their tusks and that they carry the tusks away to hide them. What is more, tusks have been found smashed against rocks.

Cynthia Moss, *Portraits in the Wild: Behaviour Studies of East African Mammals*, Boston: Houghton Mifflin, 1975

The corpse belonged to a bull which had been shot in the farm nearest to the south of the Park while raiding some maize fields. After waiting for about twenty minutes a large group of cows and calves appeared led by a familiar tall gaunt matriarch. It was none other than Boadicea with her kinship group. It seemed at first that they would pass the corpse. Then a breath of wind carried its smell directly into their trunks. They wheeled *en masse* and cautiously and deliberately closed in on the body. Shoulder to shoulder the front rank drew nearer, ten trunks waving up and down like angry black snakes, ears in that attentive half-forward position of concern. Each individual seemed reluctant to be the first to reach the bones. They all began their detailed olfactory examination. Some pieces were rocked gently to and fro with the forefeet. Others were knocked together with a wooden clonk. The tusks excited immediate interest: they were picked up, mouthed, and passed from elephant to elephant. One immature male lifted the heavy pelvis in its trunk and carried it for fifty yards before dropping it. Another stuffed two ribs into its mouth and revolved them slowly as if he were tasting the surface with his tongue. The skull was rolled over by one elephant after another. To begin with only the largest individuals could get near the skeleton, such was the crush. Boadicea, arriving late, pushed to the centre, picked up one of the tusks, twiddled it for a minute or so, then carried it away, with the blunt end in her mouth. The rest of the group now followed, many of them carrying pieces of the skeleton, which were all dropped within about a hundred yards. Virgo was the last to leave, and catching sight of me she came close by with a rib in her mouth, and waved her trunk as she went past. It was an uncanny sight to see those elephants walking away carrying bones as if in some necromantic rite.

Iain & Oria Douglas-Hamilton, *Among the Elephants*, London: Collins & Harvill Press, 1975

A curious variation of the elephant's interest in bones is related by George Adamson in his book *Bwana Game* [Collins & Harvill Press, 1968]. He was obliged to shoot one of a party of bull elephants who had chased the District Commissioner around his own garden. The bull was shot at the scene of his misdemeanour, and, after allowing the local Turkana tribesmen to cut off as much meat as they could, Adamson had the carcass dragged about half a mile away. That night some elephants visited the body, picked up a shoulder blade and a leg bone and returned them to exactly the spot where the elephant had been shot. It was impossible to prove that they were his companions of the previous day but unless the replacement of the bones at that spot was a coincidence it seems that the place of death held some significance.

An observation of Ian Parker further supports the idea that elephants may be able to recognize the place of death even after the carcass has been totally removed. He was once herding by aircraft a small family unit during a cropping operation and they were moving steadily towards the gun party on the ground when suddenly they changed their course and headed for a discoloured patch in the soil. Parker realized that here was the fibrous content of an elephant which had been 'utilized' [euphemism for killed] three weeks previously. Despite the elephants' nervousness caused by the aircraft they all stopped when they reached the spot and made a thorough investigation with their trunks, huddling together for a few minutes before moving on to meet their fate.

Iain & Oria Douglas-Hamilton, *Among the Elephants*, London: Collins & Harvill Press, 1975

Why do elephants interest themselves deeply in a dead elephant, sometimes take the trouble to bury it, and remove and carry around tusks and bones from a skeleton? Goodness knows. These are real questions. They are real because they all have an answer. Fresh understanding of the context could illuminate them. But they do not erode the central area where we know what is going on. Difficult cases crop up in every area of inquiry; they never give ground for general scepticism. Interspecies sympathy certainly encounters some barriers. So does sympathy between human beings. But the difficulties arising here cannot possibly mean that any attempt to reach out beyond the familiar lit circle of our own lives is doomed, delusive, or sentimental.

Mary Midgley, *Beast & Man: The Roots of Human Nature*, London: Methuen, 1980

Elephants, bizarrely (but the practice is well attested), bury dead bodies. No one, to my knowledge, has yet worked out any evolutionary explanation of this. The fears and the concerns of beasts do not demonstrate that they fear or recognize death as the irrevocable end of their or others' lives . . . Only creatures who have invested emotional energy in the fulfilment of plans, or the welfare of friends, or who are metaphysically appalled by the thought of their own absence from the world, are in a position to fear death as such. Not that all our deaths are equally abhorrent. A young mother's death is tragedy; a centenarian's is not – unless we're moved to think that particular life wasted. Such assessments and obituaries mark our knowledge that death is a rite of passage, of a living person to a ghost, an ancestor. How beasts feel about their dead we do not know.

For us, the realization of our coming death may be the spur to an awakened life; our appreciation of ourselves as objects in the world may be the moment when we realize we die . . . Selfhood, in its strongest form, comes into the world as part of a social tradition of treating each individual as a separate and innately valuable entity. Not every human tradition has inculcated these values, but even traditions which do not may have to accommodate the sudden wakening that comes when we see ourselves as others see us, and do not like the sight. Mavericks may be the first individuals, the first to wonder what to do, the first not to be content with becoming a ghost in a continuing tradition. If there are maverick beasts, who knows?

Stephen R. L. Clark, *The Nature of the Beast: Are Animals Moral?*, Oxford: Oxford University Press, 1982

Of all the dumb Beasts, this creature certainly shares the most of Human Understanding: kind usage exercises their Ambition, contumely fires their Revenge.

The Learned Job Ludolphus, *A New History of Ethiopia*, London: Smith, 1682

I do not mean to call an elephant a vulgar animal; but if you think about him carefully, you will find that his non-vulgarity consists in such gentleness as is possible to elephantine nature; not in his insensitive hide, nor in his clumsy foot; but in the way he will lift his foot if a child lies in his way; and in his sensitive trunk, and still more sensitive mind, and capability of pique on points of honour.

John Ruskin, *Modern Painters*, London: Smith, Elder & Co., 1843–60

Sawmill elephants were at one time quite a show-piece in the mills where they were used, and those invited to see them were usually asked to come by twelve-thirty p.m.; for at one o'clock, when the siren blew for the mid-day break, the elephants, like the men, just downed tools. They flatly refused to place the piece of timber they were holding between tusks and trunk on the stack, but just dropped it.

J. H. Williams, *Elephant Bill*, London: Rupert Hart-Davis, 1950

On the authority of a philosopher, Hagnon of Tarsus, Plutarch [*Moralia, De Sollertia Animalium*, 12, 968] tells how an elephant in Syria, feeling that its keeper was stealing half its barley ration, carefully made two piles of it one day to make the thief aware that he knew. Another rascally keeper stole part of the ration and put stones under the remainder to make the pile look normal and deceive his master: the elephant took revenge by flinging with its trunk a mass of sand into the keeper's pot of porridge. Another story (12, 968) told how boys in Rome used to annoy an elephant by pricking its trunk with their styluses; one day the elephant seized a boy and lifted him up in his trunk, but when the spectators cried out the animal gently put the boy down, thinking that his fright was punishment enough.

H. H. Scullard, *The Elephant in the Greek and Roman World*, London: Thames & Hudson, 1974

Elephants, like human beings, like playing the fool; but being made a fool of is a very different matter.

J. H. Williams, *Bandoola*, London: Rupert Hart-Davis, 1953

He [George 'Slim' Lewis] says that when they squash a man it's just a passing whimsy or a momentary grumpiness.

'We mustn't give the impression the elephant is a vicious animal,' he told me. 'As a rule, it's the most docile and patient of all animals. It's just that it's big. When it does get angry, the effects are likely to be conclusive.'

Byron Fish, foreword to *Elephant Tramp*, by George W. 'Slim' Lewis, London: Peter Davies, 1955

Savage elephants are as rare as really wicked men, but those that are not savage sometimes give way to moments of bad temper. They are particularly liable to do so when they are in harness dragging a very heavy weight. Their most tiresome and dangerous habit at such moments is to pick up a large stick or stone with the trunk and throw it with great force and accuracy at some onlooker, particularly at someone in authority, whom they guess is responsible. One has to be prepared to jump, and jump quickly, when this happens.

A young European Assistant of my acquaintance visited the London Zoo with his mother and his sister on his first leave home. They went straight to the elephant house. After explaining all about the female elephant on view, he was emboldened to suggest: 'Shall I make her sit down?'

'*Hmit!*' he shouted, in close imitation of a Burmese *oozie*.

The elephant merely swished her tail and tickled her mouth with imaginary bananas.

'*Hmit!*' he shouted again, and, as the elephant ignored him, he grew angrier and more determined with the disobedient animal. *Hmit! hmit! hmit!*'

At last the elephant condescended to notice him, swinging her head round, cocking her ears, and eyeing him with an expression as though she were saying, 'So you come from Burma, too, do you?' Then, with lightning swiftness, she seized a lump of her dung the size of a cottage loaf and slung it at the young Assistant. It missed him, but it knocked against the wall behind them. No one laughed, but the elephant house was soon empty.

J. H. Williams, *Elephant Bill*, London: Rupert Hart-Davis, 1950

Elephants are most gentle and meek, never fighting or striking man or beast unless they are provoked; but being angered, they will take up a man in their trunk and cast him into the air like an arrow so many times as he is dead before he comes to the ground.

Edward Topsell, *The History of Four-Footed Beasts, describing the True and Lively Figure of every Beast . . . collected out of all the Volumes of C. Gesner and all other Writers of the Present Day*, London: W. Jaggard, 1607

On a recent visit to one of the African national parks I was told the story of a rash tourist who alighted from his motor-car near a quietly grazing bull elephant and offered him a bun. The elephant immediately seized him with his trunk, threw him twenty feet into the air, and then knelt on him. The man was crushed to pulp, and the elephant then turned his attention to his victim's motor-car, from which the other occupants had hastily fled. By the use of trunk, tusks, and limbs he proceeded systematically to demolish it, and did not desist until it was an unrecognizable hulk of twisted metal.

Richard Carrington, *Elephants*, London: Chatto & Windus, 1958

The Negroes also affirm that the elephants, meeting any people in the woods, never offer any violence to them; but that, if the shot levelled at them misses, they grow very wild.

Willem Bosman, *A New and Accurate Description of the Coast of Guinea, from A General Collection of the Best and Most Interesting Voyages and Travels in All Parts of the World*, London: J. Knapton & D. Midwinter, 1705

We come to a consideration of the elephant's moral qualities . . . In India, excepting the professional 'rogue', the elephant bears a spotless reputation for patience, amiability and obedience. The 'rogue' is an individual afflicted with insanity, either temporary or permanent. I know of no instance on record wherein a *normal elephant* with a *healthy mind* has been guilty of unprovoked homicide, or even of attempting it. I have never heard of an elephant in India so much as kicking, striking or otherwise injuring either human beings or other domestic animals. There have been several instances, however, of persons killed by elephants which were temporarily insane or on '*must*', and also by others permanently insane. In America several persons have been killed in revenge for ill treatment. In Brooklyn a female elephant once killed a civilian who burned her trunk with a lighted cigar. It is the misfortune but not the fault of the elephant that in advanced age or by want of necessary exercise, he is liable to be attacked by *must*, or sexual insanity, during which period he is clearly irresponsible for his acts.

So many men have been killed by elephants in this country that of late years the idea has been steadily gaining ground that elephants are naturally ill-tempered, and vicious to a dangerous extent. Under fair conditions, nothing could be further from the truth. We have seen that in the hands of the 'gentle Hindu' the elephant is safe and reliable, and never attacks man except under the circumstances already stated. In this country, however, many an elephant is at the mercy of quick-tempered and sometimes revengeful showmen who very often do not understand the temperaments of the animals under their control, and who during the travelling season are rendered perpetually ill-tempered and vindictive by reason of overwork and insufficient sleep. With such masters as these it is no wonder that occasionally an animal rebels, and executes vengeance . . . I am quite convinced that an elephant could by ill-treatment be driven to insanity, and I have no doubt that this has been done many times.

William T. Hornaday, Director of the New York Zoological Park, *The Minds and Manners of Wild Animals: A Book of Personal Observations*, New York: Scribner, 1922

Professor Grzimek [B. Grzimek, 'Ein merkwürdiges Verhalten von afrikanischen Elefanten', *Z. Tierpsychol.*, 13, 151–2, 1956] has recorded four second-hand accounts of elephants, both bulls and cows, killing human beings and later covering them with vegetation and soil. The most interesting of these accounts concerns a bull – it took place in the Albert National Park of the former Belgian Congo in 1936. A tourist approached this bull on foot with his camera. Despite warnings from a number of the National Park staff that the elephant was well known to be extremely dangerous, he persisted in his attempt to get some pictures and the bull charged. Unfortunately the man had a bad leg and was not quick enough in getting away. Just as he turned to flee the Park employee took a last snapshot.

The tourist was swiftly overtaken and the elephant smacked him down with a blow of its trunk. Eye-witnesses allege that he was dead before he hit the ground, but to make sure the elephant knelt on him and drove a tusk through his body under the shoulder blade. The survivors returned after the elephant had left and found that the tourist's body had been covered in plants. I was lucky to meet the avenger of the tourist, Professor L. Van den Berghe, who later tracked down the bull and destroyed it. It was discovered that the cause of his bad temper was a deep ulcerated wound, full of pus, in his head, which had obviously been caused by a bullet.

Iain & Oria Douglas-Hamilton, *Among the Elephants*, London: Collins & Harvill Press, 1975

An elephant can absorb a small number of bullets if they do not strike in a lethal place or if the wounds do not turn too septic. However, the animal usually shows signs of a perfectly foul temper when humans are next around, and this could account for the unsavoury reputation of the Knysna elephants.

In Kenya, whenever one was called out to kill a rogue who was proven dangerous, it was customary to inspect the body for bullet or spear scars and even postmortem it. In most cases involving aggressive pachyderms an old wound would be found somewhere, giving a permanent flesh scar or suppurating sore and inducing a mental trauma which caused it to charge on sight, instead of beating the retreat which most animals do when living in the wild.

Nick Carter, *The Elephants of Knysna*, Cape Town: Purnell, 1971

If anyone refuses to give it what it asks for, it empties its bladder and such a flood follows that a river seems to have swept into the man's house.

Cassiodorus, *Variae*, X, 30

In Uganda, one of the elephants that roamed around Paraa Lodge in the Park became so attached to human food that eventually he took to picking up cars and shaking them slightly to see what fell out. This practice proved so embarrassing for the authorities that the poor beast had to be destroyed. One could say that the animal's death was assured from the very first day he was offered a titbit by some innocent-minded but deadly visitor.

Nick Carter, *The Elephants of Knysna*, Cape Town: Purnell, 1971

Their tusks can batter through a reinforced concrete wall . . .
Ivan T. Sanderson, *The Dynasty of Abu: A History and Natural History of the Elephants and Their Relatives Past and Present*, London: Cassell, 1960

Matheny & Bacon, a firm that specialized in tearing down old buildings and salvaging the material, had a house to wreck a few blocks from our tent [in Seattle], so I took Tusko over there one day . . . I had Tusko put his forehead against the building and push. He obligingly butted it off its concrete foundation. He would have stomped it to kindling, but I felt he'd had enough treat for one day.

George W. 'Slim' Lewis, *Elephant Tramp*, London: Peter Davies, 1955

Down in Southern Annam, between Dong-Me and Krong-Pha, there were a number of herds of wild elephants which had taken it into their heads to demolish all the telegraph poles, bridges and isolated forestry stations they could find. They pulled down miles of wire and bent and twisted it to their heart's content, so that the repair-gangs had to unravel vast skeins of it and search for the rest in the bush before they could begin to put the lines into action again. As fast as they repaired the system it was damaged again, and as the months went by the unbroken rhythm of damage – repairs – damage – repairs became intolerable. Bridge-rails were twisted or pulled out, mile-stones over-turned and shifted, forestry huts robbed of their roofs and doors, barrels of cement or of coal-tar belonging to the Public Works Department were rolled along the roads and hidden all over the place – until it had gone beyond a joke and everybody had had just about enough of it.

William Bazé, *Just Elephants*, translated from the French by H. M. Burton, London: Elek Books, 1950

White walls, white temples are demolished more frequently than others. Elephants seem to have a predilection, or maybe a pet hatred, for white.

Near the valley [in Munnar, Sri Lanka], the forest officer recently laid out a new road through the jungle. The route was marked with white stones, every hundred yards. There they stood, neat and white, a rhythmically recurrent scandal to elephant feelings . . . after the first full moon no white stone was left standing. The elephants had uprooted and undone them all, each one of them, from the beginning to the end of the new jungle road.

Elisabeth Mann Borgese, *The Language Barrier: Beasts and Men*, New York: Holt, Rinehart & Winston, 1968

It was [in Tengnopal] that the elephants met the first of the bulldozers, monsters which were to become their workmates in the months and years to follow . . . late one night Major Murray Lees came to see me in our camp, in order to ask me what was likely to happen next morning, when his baby bulldozer encountered my train of elephants, going in the opposite direction. I was quite as scared that his bulldozer would make my elephants stampede, as he was that they would charge his mechanical pet and hurl it down the precipitous slope, or *khud*-side, with their tusks. I was careful not to give away, in our discussion, that my fears were more realistic than his . . .

I have been informed that in one of the stages of D.T.s the sufferer sees visions of green elephants with yellow braces. But I am sure that if elephants have D.T.s, they see bulldozers. The look on the faces of both the elephants and the *oozies* riding them, as they sidled round this yellow-painted D4 bulldozer, with a British subaltern perched upon it like an *oozie*, while it blew out a blue diesel engine exhaust from its head, was that of sufferers in the most acute stages of D.T.s, seeing things.

J. H. Williams, *Elephant Bill*, London: Rupert Hart-Davis, 1950

The august leaders of the World Bank, intent on their mission of promoting global economic development, have a large and unexpectedly stubborn problem on their hands these days – the elephant.

The bank, which uses funds from richer countries to promote development in poorer ones, has found elephant herds nibbling at bank-financed rice plantations in Sri Lanka, endangering maize-growing projects in Kenya, threatening a dam in Thailand and stomping through palm oil plantations in Malaysia.

And unlike other wildlife that can be scared off by civilization or can be airlifted to more convenient locations, the 5,000 to 10,000-pound pachyderms that range more or less freely through the Third World will not easily be moved from their normal grazing areas. Instead, in their relentless search for water and food, the earth's largest land mammals have devised a variety of ingenious ways through barriers in their way.

Electrical fences, used at several World Bank projects, only occasionally slow most herds as they move through their normal parade routes. One native farmer reported that his electronic barrier sputtered and died after a crafty modern-day mammoth uprooted a nearby tree and dropped it on the fence.

At another site, bank engineers tried protecting newly developed croplands by digging moats with steep sides – only to find that elephant 'engineers' methodically butted their heads and shovelled their big tusks against the sides of the ditches, breaking them down into gentle slopes so they could amble across to their vegetarian dinner.

'You've got to remember that this is the largest terrestrial land mammal, and its major strategy is to search for food by going from place to place,' said John Seidensticker, an ecologist and mammal expert at the National Zoological Park in Washington. 'Nothing ever holds them back for very long.'

There are numerous stories of the singleminded nature of elephants – especially the very old cows in Asia, who apparently never forget particularly delicious patches of forest and their chosen routes to get to them. Even a well-known stream that suddenly becomes a raging river will not necessarily slow the big, grey mother elephants who run their matriarchal society.

Seidensticker reported herds of elephants that walked through rivers so deep that only their trunks were sticking out, drawing in air as they crossed, like huge, fleshy submarines.

'We found recently that there have been big cost over-runs because of elephant damage,' said Robert Goodland, an environmental officer at the Bank. 'And our purpose is to find some reasonable ways of dealing with the problem.'

Forest creatures that like to move out of the trees occasionally to nibble on grasses in the fields, elephants are increasingly finding themselves trapped in pockets of forest, surrounded by human development.

'All of these problems are people-generated. It's not like the elephants are going after things, rather the encroachment is forcing elephants into different behaviour,' said Thomas E. Lovejoy, vice-president for science for the World Wildlife Fund.

Eleanor Randolph, 'Trunk line, a problem of elephantine proportions', London: *Guardian*, 5 February 1983

I have found my happiness not in considering myself as Homo Sapiens set apart from the rest of creation, but in seeing that I fit in with the rest of nature, what are called so wrongly the animal and vegetable kingdoms. I believe that plants and animals have an immediate sensitiveness, an awareness of living, of what is good and what is perilous, that we humans cut ourselves off from to our detriment. That is what the jungle has taught me.

J. H. Williams, *Bandoola*, London: Rupert Hart-Davis, 1953

We surprised an elephant on his way to the river; he gathered himself threateningly – a front view of inexpressible majesty, the pliant trunk bellicose . . . then he too swerved away, turning his untailored backview towards us, his too large baggy trousers of crinkled rubber centred by the unimpressive ropy tail: an apologetic and endearing rump . . .

As they trundle away, humped and apparently boneless, they arouse an extraordinary feeling of sympathy. They almost look as if they were human beings who had been turned into elephants by a humorous magician.

Juliette Huxley, *Wild Lives of Africa*, London: Collins, 1963

Other creatures have long, flowing hair: that of the elephant is short and soft. He differs in many other ways, too, bending at the knee like a man, having breasts near the armpit, like a woman . . .

Aretaeus, *Corpus Medicorum Craecorum*, 4, 13

They also suffer from their own form of certain diseases commonly found in human beings. These include diabetes, nettle-rash, pneumonia, peritonitis, flatulent colic, the common cold, and even mumps.

Richard Carrington, *Elephants*, London: Chatto & Windus, 1958

Primates and elephants are the only mammals that nurse their babies from two breasts which develop in the same relative position on the mother's body.

In their thinking and in their emotions, elephants are the most like human beings of any animal. Their growth to maturity and their lifespan are almost exactly the same as ours . . .

George W. 'Slim' Lewis, *Elephant Tramp*, London: Peter Davies, 1955

The cat may be divine, the lion may be royalty; the dog and the horse may be faithful yeomen; but the elephant is surely Plato's philosopher/statesman, ready, indeed eager, to cooperate with mankind for the good of creation as a whole.

F. C. Sillar & R. M. Meyler, *Elephants Ancient and Modern*, New York: Viking Press, 1968

What is Anthropomorphism? It is nonsense, I have been suggesting, to suppose that intelligence or rationality could replace instinct. And I have said that the structure of our instincts is inherited from our primate forebears, though of course with many alterations evolved by our own species. People may make a further objection to this idea, saying that the names we use for human feelings and motives – fear, anger, affection – cannot properly be used of animals at all, or that, if used, they do not carry the same sense that they do with people . . .

Now people obviously sometimes do attribute to animals feelings or motives that they do not have, treating the animals as if they were people. And this is called anthropomorphism. The ordinary use of this term, however, implies that the mistake is one of fact; there are other feelings the animal *does* have, and we can often name them. Thus the sentimental dog owner attributes affection to his pet when bystanders attribute greed. And this (it is important to note) is a difference of opinion that can occur in a human context too – the company president claims that his deputy is devoted to him; others understand the fellow's actions differently.

It is a much more extreme position to say that we would be wrong, not just in attributing affection to *this* dog, but in attributing to any dog any feeling or motive whatever. Students of animal behaviour do quite often disclaim any right to talk about the 'subjective' feelings of animals. They should consider whether they have any right to talk about the subjective feelings of people either, for the position is very similar. In no case can we *be* anybody but ourselves. We cannot 'get inside' someone else – we genuinely do not know what the exact quality of the feeling accompanying his actions is like, and would doubtless be astonished if it could somehow be conveyed to us.

Mary Midgley, *Beast & Man: The Roots of Human Nature*, London: Methuen, 1979

Animals manifested mental phenomena long before man existed . . . the elephant prefigured the sagacity of the human mind.

Robert Chambers, *Vestiges of the Natural History of Creation*, London: John Church, 1844

The 19th-century tendency towards anthropomorphism led to misunderstanding because it was not backed up with accurate observation. If today there is a move back towards attributing to animals characteristics hitherto thought exclusively human, it is because observations of animal behaviour have forced the conclusion that they do indeed possess these characteristics. The idea that there may be some sort of continuity in the mental abilities of humans and other animals has been out of favour since the turn of the century; no adequate evidence had been produced at that time. But some biologists are exploring this idea once more, influenced perhaps by the argument that since our physical evolution can be traced through lesser species, so our mental evolution should be.

In any case, it is no longer outrageous to suggest that some animals might themselves have something worth calling understanding. With the development of theories of animal behaviour that have some predictive power, we are at last in a position to claim an understanding of animals that is scientifically based . . . The hours spent watching animals in the wild now have a purpose greater than contributing to natural history. Sooner or later every sequence of observed behaviour will fit into a theoretical pattern that encompasses the entire animal kingdom . . . Once we have discovered the evolutionary criteria for the development of the sort of behavioural flexibility that can be called 'intelligence', we may well be on the way to solving the problem at the heart of our own evolution.

Georgina Ferry (ed.), *The Understanding of Animals*, Oxford: Basil Blackwell & *New Scientist*, 1984

The possibility that animals have mental experiences is often dismissed as anthropomorphic because it is held to imply that other species have the same mental experiences a man might have under comparable circumstances. But this widespread view itself contains the questionable assumption that human mental experiences are the only kind that can conceivably exist. This belief that mental experiences are a unique attribute of a single species is not only parsimonious; it is conceited. It seems more likely than not that mental experiences, like many other characters, are widespread, at least among multicellular animals, but differ greatly in nature and complexity.

Awareness probably confers a significant adaptive advantage by enabling animals to react appropriately to physical, biological and social events, and signals from the surrounding world, with which their behaviour interacts.

Opening our eyes to the theoretical possibility that animals have significant mental experiences is only a first step toward the more difficult procedure of investigating their actual nature and importance to the animals concerned. Great caution is necessary until adequate methods have been developed to gather independently verifiable data about the properties and significance of any mental experiences animals may prove to have.

It has long been argued that human mental experiences can only be detected and analysed through the use of language and introspective reports, and that this avenue is totally lacking in other species. Recent discoveries about the versatility of some animal communication systems suggest that this radical dichotomy may also be unsound. It seems possible, at least in principle, to detect and examine any mental experiences or conscious intentions that animals may have . . .

The future extension and refinement of two-way communication between ethologists and the animals they study offers the prospect of developing in due course a truly experimental science of cognitive ethology.

Donald R. Griffin, *The Question of Animal Awareness*, New York: The Rockefeller University Press, 1976

A very interesting and painstaking investigation of the mental capacity and the memorizing ability of a female elephant was made recently in a scientific institute in Germany. The elephant was presented with two boxes, one marked with a symbol known to her to be 'negative' (meaning the box contained no food and was not in any other way desirable) and the other marked with a 'neutral' symbol which meant the box might or might not contain something. After a few trials the elephant, it is stated, 'became much *annoyed*, but usually chose the neutral, just in case.'

These would at first sight appear to be incautious words to use in a scientific report, and the word 'annoyed' in particular would seem to be wholly unscientific, for it is not proper to impute human feelings to animals. It is true that one of the commonest reactions of any animal *seems* to be to get 'annoyed'. However, the experimenters had apparently neither poked a stick at the elephant nor consummated the ultimate insult of laughing at her, nor had they deprived her of something desirable. Moreover, the subject became annoyed *before* making her selection and not after. Her anger was not due to making a wrong choice. She knew perfectly well, by hundreds of past experiments over a period of months, that one of the boxes definitely did *not* contain the desired object, and she also knew that the other might or might not. Her peeve was apparently with the nature of the experiment, *not* with its result.

The elephant concerned displayed emotions that were hardly, if at all, distinguishable from what our own would have been in the same circumstances.

Ivan T. Sanderson, *The Dynasty of Abu: A History and Natural History of the Elephants and Their Relatives Past and Present*, London: Cassell 1960

The elephant is never won with anger.

John Wilmot, Earl of Rochester, *Valentinian*, I, i, *c.* 1679, in *Collected Works of John Wilmot, Earl of Rochester*, ed. John Hayward, London: The Nonesuch Press, 1926

The friendship an elephant shows its trainer is hard to explain to people who have had no experience with it. You carry on conversations, some of them spoken and some by a sort of telepathy. Elephants rumble from their throats or chirp through the trunk when talking. They also gain attention by rapping the ground with their trunks, which gives off a hollow, metallic sound.

An elephant meets you on equal terms. He makes up his own mind about individual persons. He doesn't love you unless you love him. Give him abuse and he will hand it back when his chance comes. Gain his confidence and he will be your friend for life. An elephant that trusts his handler can be led through fire, but his trust must be won first.

I have met only one elephant whose confidence I couldn't gain when I really worked towards that goal. His name was Ziggy, and he'd become soured on the world and all men. He did his best to kill me, but long before he tried it I knew what was going to happen, because an elephant hand learns to know what his charge is thinking.

George W. 'Slim' Lewis, *Elephant Tramp*, London: Peter Davies, 1955

The fact that men and elephants live about as long as one another and come to maturity at much the same ages means that they can live together all their lives. They can thus acquire a lifelong mutual knowledge of each other's characters. With no other domestic animal is this possible. A baby boy may be born in an elephant camp, and at the same moment an elephant calf may be being born a mile or two away in the jungle; and that child and that calf may grow up together, play together, work together all their working lives, and they may still be familiar friends when sixty years have passed.

J. H. Williams, *Elephant Bill*, London: Rupert Hart-Davis, 1950

However much you come to know about elephants or however well trained your animal is, you will remain a slave to it as long as you two shall be together. The elephant will work for you and with you and on occasion, in show business, it will literally lead you through your routine and through life. Almost daily some trained elephant comes to the aid of its human friend, unasked and uninstructed. Many a man has been beaten to a pulp or hurled into the branches of a tree for attacking or even threatening a mahout, a trainer, or a zoo keeper. During the war, elephants faced gunfire to rescue their oozies and smashed down burning buildings to rescue people. More than once elephants have handled hoses at circus fires, but I have never heard of anybody *teaching* one to do so. Elephants think; and they think of *us*; they have compassion as well as a mere desire to protect their human friends. In return they ask only this – *that you devote your entire life to them.*

Ivan T. Sanderson, 'Of Bread and Circuses' in *The Dynasty of Abu: A History and Natural History of the Elephants and Their Relatives Past and Present*, London: Cassell, 1960

Sometimes an elephant will show its intelligence by divining what its *oozie* wishes.

A case I remember concerned an animal which would not work with a rider on his head, but was obedient to the words of command given by his *oozie* walking alongside. I was watching this beast straightening logs in a creek – that is to say, placing them in rows of eight or twelve parallel to each other and pointing down the bed of the stream, in readiness for the first floods to carry them away. The *oozie* was sitting on the bank; work was almost finished, but, because I was around, he knew every log had to be straight in line with the others before they broke off.

There was one noticeable and unshapely log, and the elephant came to the last row in which it lay. He was a big tusker, and was doing all the work with his tusks and head, free of all chains. Without any word of command being given, he let the first log alone, and began shifting the second, keeping one eye on his *oozie*, as though saying: 'Come on, wake up and tell me what you want!'

The *oozie* soon told him, shouting: 'You old son of a bitch! What's wrong with that one? Leave it.'

The elephant moved on to the next log, keeping his eye cocked on his *oozie*, like an old man looking over a pair of spectacles.

'No,' shouted the *oozie*. 'You know as well as I do,' and made a gesture of picking up a stone to throw at his beast.

The elephant gave a squeal of pure delight at having pulled his *oozie*'s leg, and, without hesitation, disregarded the next five logs and, without pausing, bent down and rolled the one irregularly placed log over four times, leaving it exactly parallel with the others and about a foot from them. Then he walked up to his master, as though to say: 'Enough fooling, let's break off!' and the day's work was finished for man and beast.

J. H. Williams, *Elephant Bill*, London: Rupert Hart-Davis, 1950

Each time, Po Toke [Bandoola's *oozie*] indicated what he was going to ask Bandoola to do, then silently conveyed his wishes to the animal, whose powers of differentiation were quite remarkable. We saw him respond to a series of unspoken instructions . . . There have been many arguments about the intelligence of elephants; but this demonstration, and all the other exhibitions of their cleverness that I had seen in the jungle, convinced me that Jim's [Elephant Bill's] theory that the elephant is the most intelligent animal in the world was true.

Susan Williams, *The Footprints of Elephant Bill*, London: William Kimber, 1962

'Up in Kerala,' the chief mahout, who spoke some English, said, 'a friend of mine, a mahout, he drank a lot . . . When he was on a binge, he'd pass out. Then his elephant would pick him up, gently, with his trunk round the waist – and he'd carry him home and put him down before his house door. That's the smartest thing I've ever seen an elephant do.' He had a challenging look on him, as if he really wanted to say, 'He was much smarter than you fools who drink – he'd carry you all home any time.'

Elisabeth Mann Borgese, *The Language Barrier: Beasts and Men*, New York: Holt, Rinehart & Winston, 1968

I have known one case of something that seemed like remorse in an elephant. He was a tusker who killed his rider. But he guarded the body, and would let nobody get near it, for a whole week. He grazed all round it, and charged in mad fury at anyone who came near. When the body had quite decomposed he wandered away from it, and ten days later was recaptured, without any difficulty, and behaved quite normally. He was not on *musth*.

J. H. Williams, *Elephant Bill*, London: Rupert Hart-Davis, 1950

In December 1975 it was reported in the Press that Sandra, a twenty-five-year-old circus elephant, in Pisa, went on 'hunger strike' after her companion and trainer married. According to one report, on her last appearance she played the piano with her trunk and danced a little waltz, became too weak to carry on and died of a broken heart, 'in spite of intravenous injections and a jar of honey.'

Maurice Burton, *Just Like an Animal*, London: J. M. Dent, 1978

Monotheism does have a relatively hospitable side, a tradition in which animals can be seen as fellow-servants of God, or as aspects of his glory. But it has also a sharply exclusive and destructive side, in which the Lord tolerates no rival for our regard. In this mood, the church often and explicitly insisted that all plants and animals must be viewed merely as objects given to man as his instruments, that to have any sort of regard for them in themselves was sinful and superstitious folly. What is interesting is that many of those scientific humanists who most sternly rejected Christianity have continued this second tradition – but with man himself taking the place of the jealous God. Thus Marx in the *Grundrisse* said that 'the great civilizing influence of capitalism' lay in its rejection of the 'deification of nature'. Thus it was that 'nature becomes for the first time simply an object for mankind, purely a matter of utility'.

Mary Midgley, *Beast & Man: The Roots of Human Nature*, Brighton: Harvester, 1979

It is something of a problem to dispose of an elephant that has died or been killed in captivity, on account of its weight, but generally it is cut up for its fat, and as meat for the big cats.

George W. 'Slim' Lewis, *Elephant Tramp*, London: Peter Davies, 1955

Take an elephant's foot, preferably young and very fresh; remove the white flesh which covers the bone, and cut it into strips the thickness of your finger, reminding one of sticks of *pâté de guimauve*. Place the appetising strips for two days in the sun to dry, and collect the pure fat which exudes from them in the form of clear oil. To make the dish known as *mwendo wa nzou*, take one of these strips, cut it into small pieces, put it into a saucepan containing a little water, place it on a gentle fire, and renew the water several times. When a jelly has formed, add to it the oil in which you have browned a few onions, a little thyme, etc., or an equivalent aromatic plant, one or two very strong chillies, and let it cook for twenty hours, still adding water when necessary. Serve hot, with manioc flour or grated biscuit separately.

N.B. – This dish keeps several days, and only requires re-warming.

Edouard Foa, *After Big Game in Central Africa*, London, 1899

In a country such as Zambia, which has in places a chronic shortage of protein, it would be politically and morally unacceptable to kill a large number of elephants and then to leave the meat in the field. Accordingly it was decided that all the carcasses should be processed for human consumption. From consultations with the retail trade on what would be the most readily marketable form for the product, it became evident that frozen fillets of elephant meat would be preferable to canned or the traditional smoke-dried products. What is more, the Veterinary Department in Zambia made it clear that all the elephant meat must pass the standard meat inspection procedure, whether sold in town or given away free. Consequently, a centrally situated abattoir had to be built, incorporating a deep-freeze chamber, to which the elephants killed in the field could be transported for processing.

John Hanks, participant in the culling of 1,464 elephants in the South Game Reserve in Luangwa, 1965–69, *A Struggle for Survival: The Elephant Problem*, London: Country Life Books, 1979

The normal and appropriate relationship between humans and wild animals is . . . one of distance. It is difficult in the context of the zoo, with the enforced closeness of the animals, to maintain truly wild animals.

A further transformation of the animals occurs if humans are allowed to engage in direct physical contact with them. For if the animal is not to flee from such an encounter, it must be accustomed to human contact, that is to say, it must be tamed. The human experience of such a creature destroys its authenticity (a quality which is linked to its independence) as a wild animal.

Bob Mullan & Garry Marvin, *Zoo Culture*, London: Weidenfeld & Nicolson, 1987

Elephants have a wonderful love to their own country, and, although they might be ever so well delighted with divers foods and joys in other places, yet in memory of their country they send forth tears.

Edward Topsell, *The History of Four-Footed Beasts, describing the True and Lively Figure of every Beast . . . collected out of all the Volumes of C. Gesner and all other Writers of the Present Day*, London: W. Jaggard, 1607

Whether they like it or not zoos are in the business of trading animals . . . Giraffes do not naturally belong in the middle of Tokyo, nor polar bears in Washington and certainly not lions in Copenhagen, but unfortunately for them humans seem to need them there and, furthermore, can command them to be there. In zoos man has been able to go beyond nature and transform it, to alter the natural distribution of animal species such that there are now populations of animals existing completely outside their natural environment. This relationship of the human to the animal world has taken different shades of meaning in different cultures and different eras but, at the most basic level, zoos are institutions of power, in that they reflect the uniquely human ability to hold in captivity and dominate large numbers of diverse wild animals for the purpose of human enjoyment and human benefit. The zoo constitutes a gallery of images constructed by man. The fact that he is able to arrange around him living creatures from all parts of the world, to make decisions with regard to the quality and conditions of their lives and to give shape to the world for them in terms of his imagination and desire is, in the end, an expression of power.

Bob Mullan & Garry Marvin, *Zoo Culture*, London: Weidenfeld & Nicolson, 1987

Queen Victoria routinely consigned to the Zoological Society the 'stream of barbaric offerings in the shape of lions, tigers, leopards, &c, which is continually flowing from tropical princes' [*Quarterly Review*, 98: 245, 1855], and her eldest son followed suit, donating not only animals he accumulated when touring the outposts of Empire as Prince of Wales, but also gifts such as the five lions and two zebras he received from Emperor Menelik of Abyssinia on his coronation as Edward VII. If the royal family considered the London Zoo a metaphorical extension of its private domains, so too, although doubtless in an attenuated sense, did many ordinary visitors to Regent's Park. After the governing council abolished admission restrictions, the zoo emerged as a national public institution, which reflected its glory on all British citizens. And this glory was not solely political or military, whether represented by animals that had been captured in the field, or those that had been presented to the Queen as a tribute, or those that had been adopted at exotic postings as regimental pets and then relinquished to the zoo when they grew unmanageable. In a more pragmatic sense the zoo illustrated Britain's economic prowess, the variety of the animals was 'a proof that our commerce is pushed to the ends of the earth!' [F. G. Aflalo, *A Walk through the Zoological Gardens*, London: Sands, 1900]. Even the scientific side of the zoo testified to the superior competence of Britons, who were able to maintain so many exotic species in confinement and to manipulate and study them, so that they were better understood and appreciated than by the peoples who had lived among them for millennia . . .

As the emblem of British domination over its colonial empire, the London Zoo also inevitably came to symbolize Britain's competition for pre-eminence with western rivals. Helping to stock it became a quasi-official duty for consuls and other colonial officials, whose frequent gifts were recorded with gratitude in the Zoological Society's proceedings. From the beginning the London Zoo was measured against its European competitors. Indeed, a primary motive for its establishment had been Britain's shameful lack of an institution for the study of living exotic animals, despite being 'richer than any other country in the extent and variety of our possessions', while its neighbours could boast 'magnificent institutions' devoted to this purpose [John Bastin, 'The First Prospectus of the Zoological Society of London: A New Light on the Society's

Origins', *Journal of the Society for the Bibliography of Natural History*, 5, 370–2, 1970]. Cause for embarrassment quickly faded, however. Soon after it was stocked, the Zoological Society's menagerie was proclaimed 'the most extensive assemblage of living Quadrupeds and Birds ever exhibited in this, or perhaps any other, country'; after a few decades it was without question 'the finest public Vivarium in Europe' [E. T. Bennett, *The Gardens and Menageries of the Zoological Society Delineated*, Chiswick: T. Tegg & N. Hailes, 1830; John Timbs, *Curiosities of London*, London: David Bogue, 1829]. But the struggle continued, the society's judges never allowed it to rest comfortably on its considerable laurels. When, for example, the first live pandas appeared in zoos elsewhere in Europe, *Nature* goaded Regent's Park to a parallel act of symbolic acquisition: 'As France and Russia can now both boast of specimens, England, whose interests in China are so predominant, surely ought to be able to obtain some likewise.'

This competitive national pride was insulted in 1882, when P. T. Barnum, the American entrepreneur, arranged to purchase Jumbo, an enormous African elephant who had been for many years the pride of Regent's Park. Many of the children who had ridden on his back, as well as their parents, felt personally bereft when they heard of his projected departure. (Ironically, the Council of the Zoological Society decided to sell Jumbo because he was becoming difficult to control; zoo administrators feared an accident, something they were reluctant to reveal at the time of the sale.) There was a public outcry, including letters to the editor criticizing the sale as 'a disgrace to English lovers of animals', and an attempt orchestrated by the *Daily Telegraph* to get Barnum to cancel his purchase for an offered £100,000 (about one hundred times the best guess of the purchase price). But in the voluminous pamphlet literature that registered this national trauma, humanitarian concerns were incontestably secondary to those of patriotism. The problem was not that Jumbo would suffer under the big top, but that the United States had managed to wrest him from Britain. In one such doggerel, entitled *The Farewell of the Zoo Pet*, Jumbo assured his fans that 'I love old England's dear little girls and boys', in another he announced that 'I love the brave old British flag, of it my boys I'll always brag/And you must clearly understand, I do not care for Yankee land.' Jumbo was a valued chattel, and the British public had a hard time giving him up to a transatlantic rival.

Harriet Ritvo, *The Animal Estate: The English and Other Creatures in the Victorian Age*, Cambridge, Mass.: Harvard University Press, 1987

She [Pole Pole] doesn't have a perfect life . . . As with human beings, there are all sorts of people who don't have the lives they might have.

Dr Brian Bertram, Curator of Mammals, London Zoo, quoted in the *Observer*, 16 October 1983

In the night time they seem to lament with sighs and tears their captivity and bondage, but if any come like unto modest persons they refrain suddenly, and are ashamed to be found either murmuring or sorrowing.

Edward Topsell, *The History of Four-Footed Beasts, describing the True and Lively Figure of every Beast . . . collected out of all the Volumes of C. Gesner and all other Writers of the Present Day*, London: W. Jaggard, 1607

The sight of a majestic elephant in chains, so obviously restricted in his movements, dampened my initial ardour for that outing [to Belle Vue Zoo in Manchester] . . . Elephants are part of a roaming, social herd. Their natural habitat involves travel over great distances in search of food and contact. Confinement in an alien environment cannot but lead to cruelty and suffering. This unnatural aspect of animal imprisonment applies to the overwhelming number of species to be found in zoos. Protection from enemies, and the removal of the quest for food, inevitably release the animals from their natural activity in the wild. Strong, deep instincts are frustrated. Chronic anxiety, boredom, and various manifestations of psychological disturbance can and do result from this confinement.

Roland Boyes, 'Lobbying for Parliament', in *Beyond the Bars: The Zoo Dilemma*, Virginia McKenna, Will Travers & Jonathan Wray (eds), Wellingborough: Thorsons, 1987

Our present (1921) male African elephant, Kartoum, is not . . . hostile toward people, but his insatiable desire is to break and to smash all of his environment that can be bent or broken. His ingenuity in finding ways to damage doors and gates, and to bend or to break steel beams is amazing. His greatest feat consisted in breaking squarely in two, by pushing with his head, a 90-pound steel railroad iron used as the top bar of his fence. He knows the mechanism of the latch of the ponderous steel door between his two box stalls . . .

Kartoum has gone over every inch of surface of his two apartments, his doors, gates and fences, to find something that he can break or damage. The steel linings of his apartment walls, originally five feet high, we have been compelled to extend upward to a height of nine feet, to save the brick walls from being battered and disfigured. He has searched his steel fences throughout, in order to find their weakest points, and concentrate his attacks upon them. If the sharp-pointed iron spikes three inches long that are set all over his doors are perfectly solid, he respects them, but if one is the least bit loose in its socket, he works at it until he finally breaks it off.

William T. Hornaday, Director of the New York Zoological Park, *The Minds and Manners of Wild Animals: A Book of Personal Observations*, New York: Scribners, 1922

Death of Elephants in London Zoo, Regents Park, 1946–1983.
'Ranee', age 10, died, reason not recorded, 1946
'Rajah', age 12, shot – seriously injured two keepers, 1951
'Diksie', age 27, died – fell in moat, 1967
'Rusty', age 27, shot – suspected TB and foot rot, 1969
'Toto', age 20, died – lung haemorrhage and bruising, said to be result of falling in zoo moat four years earlier, 1980
'Lakshmi', age 28, transferred to Holland where she was said to have been found dead, hanging by one chained leg in moat. London Zoo says she had heart attack before falling.
'Pole Pole', age 17, killed by lethal injection when she could not get to her feet, 1983

Virginia McKenna, Will Travers & Jonathan Wray (eds), *Beyond the Bars: The Zoo Dilemma*, Wellingborough: Thorsons, 1987

Then when Toto died (again because of bad design of the house – no way of removing the body), they did the post-mortem in the next den to Pole. You cannot imagine the effect this had on her. She walked round in circles day and night for six weeks till she dropped. It was months before she settled.

Jan Adams, a keeper's fiancée, in *Beyond the Bars: The Zoo Dilemma*, Virginia McKenna, Will Travers & Jonathan Wray (eds), Wellingborough: Thorson, 1987

At present, she [a female African elephant, aged 21 years in 1988; in Edinburgh Zoo for 12 years] is being trained to accept a chain round her foot so that, when necessary, she can readily be examined by the Zoo vet.

Extract from the 75th Anniversary Commemorative Guidebook to Edinburgh Zoo, published by The Royal Zoological Society of Scotland, Murrayfield, 1988

It's good to take her ['Rani'] out from time to time. Some people don't like to see her in chains, but I think it's more 'circusy'.

Robert Raven, elephant handler, Gerry Cottle's Circus, in conversation with Heathcote Williams, Newton Abbot, 19 September 1988

For many people, circuses, and the attitude of their owners, are even more contemptible than are zoos and the conduct of their proprietors. I have before me, as I write, a cutting from *The Times* newspaper of 24 November 1986, in which Mr Richard Chipperfield of the circus family is quoted as saying, following criticism of the alleged confinement of three elephants for three months in a 40-foot by 8-foot metal container, that 'those three elephants are worth £100,000. We look after *stuff* (my italics) like that.' Comment on such an attitude, if accurately reported, would be superfluous.

Sir Christopher Lever, in the introduction to *Beyond the Bars: The Zoo Dilemma*, Virginia McKenna, Will Travers & Jonathan Wray (eds), Wellingborough: Thorsons, 1987

An elephant we had captured actually committed suicide. One evening, at a village called No Lu, we had tied up our captives as usual and retired to a neighbouring house for a meal, when one of the Emperor's men came in to inform him that a female elephant was dead. We followed him out and we could see quite clearly what had happened. The poor creature – who that afternoon had allowed herself to be tied up without protest – had voluntarily tightened the rope about her neck by walking round and round the great trunk and then, when it was as tight as she could get it, had thrown herself forward on to her knees and strangled herself.

William Bazé, *Just Elephants*, translated from the French by H. M. Burton, London: Elek Books, 1955

They know their strength, but they don't use it aggressively and they abhor fighting or physical violence of any kind. Most of them show noticeable signs of revulsion to bloodshed or death in any form and display distress in face of these things.

Ivan T. Sanderson, *The Dynasty of Abu: A History and Natural History of the Elephants and Their Relatives Past and Present*, London: Cassell, 1960

Naturalists assure us that all animals are sagacious in proportion as they are removed from the tyranny of others. In native liberty, the elephant is a citizen, the beaver an architect; but whenever the tyrant man intrudes upon their community, their spirit is broken, they seem anxious only for safety, and their intellects suffer an equal diminution with their property.

Oliver Goldsmith, *An Enquiry into the Present State of Polite Learning*, London: R. & J. Dodsley, 1759

The extraordinary development of the Roman taste for bloody spectacles may have been due to a self-conscious idea that such sights were right and proper for a martial people. But when this development had once begun, it continued because the nobles were competitively interested in pleasing the public which could elect them to magistracies, and also because it might be taken as a distinction in itself, or *dignitas*, to outdo others, or not to be outdone, in the entertainment which one gave one's fellow-citizens; while an expanding empire was furnishing the means of appealing to the public taste in novel ways, and the aristocracy could use the "patronage" (*patrocinium*) which it exercised over the more or less subject allies of Rome to induce them to contribute to the entertainment of the Roman People. In this way it came about that in the *venationes* [spectacles of killing wild animals] of the Roman Circus, foreign animals were seen more and more frequently from the end of the third century B.C., especially "African beasts" . . .

George Jennison, *Animals for Show and Pleasure in Ancient Rome*, Manchester: Manchester University Press, 1937

Mass excitement induced by scenes of violent conflict, particularly those in which human dexterity and courage in mastering the beasts (as in Spanish bullfights today) stirred the enthusiasm of the [Roman] crowds . . . in the written sources the numbers of animals slaughtered on specific occasions are recorded cold-bloodedly and, indeed, as a matter of congratulation. In the twenty-six *venationes bestiarum Africanarum* given by Augustus, 3,500 creatures died (*Res gestae* XXII).

A very few protests raised against such scenes of sadistic barbarity are recorded in the literary sources, the most important being that of the Roman populace itself at the show given by Pompey in 55 BC (Elder Pliny, *Naturalis Historia*, VIII, 7(20,21); Dio Cassius XXXIX, 38, 2–4; Seneca, *De Brevitate Vitae* 13,6).

On this occasion 20 or 17 elephants, according to Pliny, 18 in Seneca's and Dio Cassius' version of the incident, were set to fight in the Circus against men armed with javelins, Gaetulians, so Pliny states. In Pliny's account one elephant delighted the spectators by the extraordinary fight that it put up, crawling on its knees, when its feet were wounded, to attack its opponents, whose shields it seized and tossed in the air in such a way that as they fell they formed a circle on the ground round it – *decidentia . . . erant in orbem circumiecta*; it was more like watching a clever juggler than an infuriated beast – *velut arte non furore beluae iacerentur*. The crowd was also amazed at seeing another elephant killed by a single blow when a javelin hit it below the eye and penetrated to the head's vital parts. But, when the whole troupe tried to stampede and break down the iron bars enclosing it, the onlookers were thoroughly alarmed; and their compassion and disgust were aroused when the creatures, losing all hope of escape, began to trumpet piteously and beg for mercy, running round the arena and raising their trunks heavenwards in lamentation, according to Dio's description of the scene. Dio further says that they gave the impression of calling for vengeance on their keepers, who had broken the promise made to them before they embarked in Africa that no harm should come to them. At any rate, to quote Pliny's words, the whole crowd wept and rose to its feet, cursing Pompey for his cruelty: *flens universus [populus] consurgeret dirasque Pompeio imprecaretur*. The story thus vividly told by Pliny and Dio is confirmed by Cicero's contemporary reference to Pompey's exhibition. 'The last day of the shows was devoted to the elephants. This stirred the people's wonder, but did not please them at all. In fact, it ended in their pitying the beasts and in their feeling that a certain affinity exists between men and elephants' (Cicero, *Ad Familiares*, VII, 1, 3). 'What pleasure can a cultivated man find in seeing a noble beast run through by a hunting spear?' is Cicero's comment on the general treatment of animals at the shows (Cicero, ibid.).

This is unfortunately the first and last public protest of which we have knowledge. No doubt many cultured and humane individuals were, like Cicero, disgusted by the senseless wounding and slaughtering of beasts, who, as Plutarch sharply remarks, were either forced to make a stand and fight against their will or destroyed without possessing any natural means of self-defence (Plutarch, *De Sollertia Animalium*, 7). But the horrifying spectacles of carnage still went on, at any rate in Rome; and if provincial shows involved less bloodshed, the same animals being exhibited on several successive occasions, considerations of expense, rather than feeling for the creatures, may well have been the reason. Our problem still remains.

J. M. C. Toynbee, *Animals in Roman Life and Art*, London: Thames & Hudson, 1973

In Somaliland, one of the favourite amusements was riding out, mounted on light Somali ponies, to bait wild elephants. Their *shikaries* would perhaps locate a couple of the animals in a small clump of trees, where they were resting during the heat of the day. One of the party would then ride up and fire a pistol at one of them. The result, of course, would be a scream of rage, and a furious charge by the insulted animal. Horse and rider would at once make themselves scarce. The elephant would seldom charge more than 100 yards or so away from cover, but at that distance, or under, would halt and then slowly return, thus giving another member of the party a chance. With a wild shout another horse and rider would gallop at full speed across the elephant's path, just out of reach. Round would come the huge beast in another attempt to put an end to what it justly considered a nuisance – an attempt foredoomed to failure. One after another the horsemen would gallop up to the now thoroughly infuriated beast, shouting and firing pistols, provoking ugly rushes first at one and then another of them – for all the world like a lot of schoolboys playing touch. Sometimes one or other of them had a narrow escape, but somebody would nip in at the critical moment and divert the elephant's attention. A slip or a fall would have meant a horrible death from the feet and tusks of the enraged pachyderm; but the ponies were as agile as their riders, and enjoyed the fun every whit as much.

A. Arkell-Hardwick, *An Ivory Trader in North Kenya: The Record of an Expedition through Kikuyu to Galla-land in East Equatorial Africa, with an Account of the Rendili and Burkeneji Tribes*, London, New York & Bombay: Longmans Green, 1903

It was during the invasion of German East Africa [formerly Tanganyika] that the elephant was the object of the most brutal, unsportsmanlike attack civilisation could provide. Some of the young aviators among the British forces conceived the idea of dropping bombs on an elephant herd and gathering up the ivory afterward. A plane was flown over a near-by group of elephants, the bombs struck their mark, exploded, killed a number of elephants outright, and left others groaning and helpless on the ground. Very little of the ivory was worth anything; most of it had been blown to bits along with the animals that had carried it.

E. D. Moore, *Ivory: Scourge of Africa*, London & New York: Harper & Brothers, 1931

Big game hunting, the most atavistic and antagonistic connection between humans and animals, became the fitting emblem of the new style in which the English dominated both the human and the natural worlds.

Harriet Ritvo, *The Animal Estate: The English and Other Creatures in the Victorian Age*, Cambridge, Mass.: Harvard University Press, 1987

Game Licence fees per animal charged to hunters in Zimbabwe:
Elephant (Bulls) US$ 2,800.00
Elephant (Cows) US$ 1,000.00

Magazine of the East African Wild Life Society, 5: 4, Nairobi, July/August 1982

'Big-game hunting' was and still is regarded as a 'sport', and almost everybody who could afford a rifle and a trip to East Africa has indulged in it. It began with the Boers in South Africa in the 1600's and it has continued until today.

To many people the very word 'elephant' still prompts an involuntary mental, if not actual, grab for a gun or other weapon of destruction.

Ivan T. Sanderson, *The Dynasty of Abu: A History and Natural History of the Elephants and Their Relatives Past and Present*, London: Cassell, 1960

When I went into the jungle for the first time, I had highly-coloured ideas of man-eating tigers and charging wild tusker elephants. But after a

PERILS OF THE AFRICAN JUNGLE.

comparatively short time I came to realize that the wild beasts of the jungle were not my natural enemies. They had no desire to attack me and I had no desire to attack them.

J. H. Williams, *Bandoola*, London: Rupert Hart-Davis, 1953

Once again the approach was easy. The herd was scattered about in an isolated patch of by no means dense bush in fairly open country. A little caution was needed when entering the bush to ensure that we did not stampede any of the cows in our search for the big tuskers. Eventually, after about twenty somewhat anxious minutes moving carefully around looking for them, we found them under a large tree some small distance from the main body of the herd.

The leader, a fine beast, had two big companions under the tree with him and I could see a number of other good tuskers scattered about here and there. They would be the leaders of the various families that made up the herd, whilst the old man under the tree would be the master bull that all would follow. If I could drop him in his tracks I stood a very good chance of making a big bag here, since the other bulls would not know that he was dead and would await his signal to give them the line of retreat.

I again closed in to within fifteen or twenty paces before firing. The big chap was facing me, the two others were more or less broadside on. I took the frontal brain shot and the big fellow sank down without a murmur, all four 'knees' giving way simultaneously so that he remained in an upright position, his tusks supporting his head. As the other that was facing me threw up his trunk, I shot him at the base of the throat and grabbed my second rifle. The third bull was twisting around in an undecided manner; I waited my chance and blew out his brains when he offered me a fair shot.

Out of the corner of my eye I had noticed a good deal of movement amongst the remainder of the herd whilst I had been dealing with the big chap and his companions. That, of course, was to be expected. But there was no indication of a stampede. Ears out and trunks up, they were clustered in family parties each awaiting the signal from their respective leaders, and the leaders awaiting the word from the master bull. Not getting it, they were undecided what to do. This was what I had banked on. I moved quietly around from one party to another picking out the best and dropping them. At first the different groups would rush off a little distance and then stop again, but as the shooting continued they became completely demoralized and just stood around in dismay – they had been let down by the master bull, they had apparently been abandoned by their own leaders, they just didn't know what to do about it.

I dare say I could have wiped out the greater number of them had I wished, but such, of course, was not my intention. I killed eleven of them and then was satisfied. If there were fifty or sixty of the herd to start with that was not too many in view of the long years of immunity they had enjoyed during which they had been raiding the wretched natives' food-crops to their hearts' content. Such a herd could cause positive devastation in the course of a single night's raiding. It is not the amount they eat – though that is bad enough in all conscience – but the amount they trample down and utterly destroy.

Having cut off the tails we started the return to camp amidst great jubilation. Our first day's hunting having proved so successful was a splendid omen and augured well for the remainder of the expedition. But we were not yet finished with the elephant. It was getting along towards sundown and we were all a trifle leg weary when, within a long mile of camp, we suddenly heard an elephant's tummy rumbling and his ears flop against his shoulders. The sounds were coming from a fairly dense patch of shady bush. I snicked forward the safety catch and headed straight for the place whence the rumbling had come. There

were two quite nice bulls standing with their heads together easy in the shade of a tall tree.

One bull was practically facing me; I was satisfied with his position, but wanted the other to come around a bit. So, with my lips almost touching Nasib's [Nasib-bin-Risik, his head gun-bearer] ear, I just breathed a word. He, knowing, stooped and picked up a couple of dry twigs. Gently he cracked one. In the absolute stillness that followed, huge ears swung out till they stood at right angles to the head – the bulls were listening. Again a twig cracked. Slowly, ponderously, and in absolute silence except for the faintest rustling of his hide against something, the monster moved around. And then, as he exposed his broadside, I slammed a heavy slug into his brain, bringing him down instantly. The crashing roar of the rifle was drowned in the trumpeting yell of the second bull as he threw up his trunk in alarm. But I gave him no chance to do anything. I fired the left barrel into his chest, which caused his hindquarters to give way so that he squatted there like a huge hog whilst I exchanged rifles with Nasib. But there was no need to waste another shell. He made but one effort to get to his feet, found it hopeless, and resigned himself to his end.

John Taylor ('Pondoro'), *African Rifles & Cartridges: The experiences and opinions of a professional ivory hunter with some thirty years of continuous living in the African Bush – who has used all of the various calibers and most of the suitable cartridges, and with them killed the many species of big game found on the continent of Africa*, Highland Park, New Jersey: The Gun Room Press, 1948 (reprinted 1977)

Most men who have shot elephants come afterwards to regret having done so . . .

J. H. Williams, *Elephant Bill*, London: Rupert Hart-Davis, 1950

Owing to constant hunting, many game animals have completely changed their whole character in the last fifty years. During the turn of the century, some animals were easy to hunt. To-day, they are much more cunning and dangerous. I am thinking particularly of elephants. They have learned that man is their enemy and are not as trusting as they once were . . . In those days, elephants lived mainly in open country. As they had never been hunted, they had little fear of man. A hunter could lie out in the veldt with a light rifle and pick his shots. There was little danger of a charge. Now elephants live in bush. They know more about guns than many hunters and have learned how to set ambushes. When an elephant knows he is being hunted and finds that he cannot throw the man off his spoor, he may set out to 'hunt the hunter'. At such times, an elephant is exceedingly dangerous, especially if he has been hunted before and knows something of men and their ways.

It did happen once that an elephant waited for me beside a trail after I had killed his two companions. I was lucky to kill him before he killed me, but most elephants simply seek to escape . . .

J. A. Hunter, *Hunter*, London: Hamish Hamilton, 1952

By 1973 the last population of the Bush Elephant (*Loxodonta africana africana*) in the Republic of Rwanda comprised two small groups of *c.* 70 animals each. Both were surrounded by expanding human settlements which caused rising conflict between Elephants and Man. Eventually the elephants' removal became imperative. Adults (103) and unweaned immatures (3) were therefore shot.

J. C. Haigh, I. S. C. Parker, D. A. Parkinson, & A. L. Archer, 'An Elephant Extermination', *Environmental Conservation*, 6: 4, Switzerland: The Foundation for Environmental Conservation, Winter 1979. (From the introduction: 'The authors were members of the field team that carried out the project.')

Concern has been expressed that the magnificent *Acacia albida* are being de-barked at a rate that threatens their existence. Viljoen [P. J. Viljoen, scientific observer of the desert elephants of Namibia] found that in the Hoanib River, where the largest concentration of elephants occurs, 14 per cent of the total amount of winter thorns were dead. Of these 18 per cent had been killed by elephants, mostly by ring-barking them, while the rest had died as a result of either floodwaters or fire. However he found that 26 per cent of all winter thorns consisted of established young trees. In other words their rate of regeneration more than compensated for the rate of attrition. By comparing aerial photographs taken in 1963 and 1982 and counting the number of trees per hectare, the difference was found to be negligible. His research had shown that for at least the last twenty years there is no sign that the elephants have been destroying one of the region's most important shade and food trees.

On the other hand, in season, the elephants consume great quantities of acacia seed pods which pass through their digestive system – a process that softens the seed's hard testa thereby greatly facilitating their germination. The seeds are then deposited in an immense warm nutritious pile of dung – a most auspicious start in life. When the rains come the seeds in the elephant dung are ready to germinate immediately and so get the full advantage of the rain as opposed to seeds in the pods, which must weather for a long period before the water is able to penetrate the hard testa. Tests have shown that seeds in elephant dung have a germination success rate as high as 75 per cent whereas seeds taken from the pod achieve only 12 per cent. So quite unwittingly the elephants play an important role in replacing the trees they destroy.

Mitch Reardon, *War, Drought, Poaching in the Namib Desert*, London: Collins, 1986

Some plants that have been stripped by elephants for millenia have reacted to the treatment by coating their seeds with rinds thick enough to withstand a prolonged soaking in the digestive juices. The paradoxical consequence has been that now, unless the rind is weakened by passing through an elephant, the seeds are unable to germinate at all.

David Attenborough, *Life on Earth*, London: Collins & BBC Publications, 1979

Each elephant population has a cultural knowledge of its environment, which is passed on from generation to generation. This may include such information as where to find water in the event of a severe drought – an event which may only happen once in decades, and may involve migrating to another area.

Thus, to protect elephants, a detailed knowledge of their movements over several decades is required before park boundaries are finally gazetted. This has seldom been the case, and so elephants restricted by man-made boundaries may consistently attempt to leave their park. When the park is hemmed in by agriculture, they are then branded 'crop raiders' and may be legally shot.

Petition to Upgrade the African Elephant from Threatened to Endangered Status, Washington, D.C.: The International Wildlife Coalition, December 1988

Elephants make up for the damage they do to woodlands by scattering seeds and fertilising them.
Diane Lieberman and colleagues from the University of North Dakota and the World Wide Fund for Nature examined the elephant dung found in Bia National Park, Ghana. They found that the elephants had eaten fruit and the seeds passed through them unharmed. The elephants carried seeds from 11 species of trees to different parts of the park and dropped them in their dung. The researchers also discovered that the dung greatly improved the number of seeds germinating for some species. Three in particular, *Balanites wilsoniana*, *Diospyros*, and *Pycnanthos angolensis* would not germinate in the laboratory without dung. Other species, once germinated, grew more vigorously in the dung (*Biotropica*, vol. 19, p. 35). In the Luangwa Valley, in Zambia, the *Scelerocarpya caffra* tree is a favourite food of the elephants. They eat the fruits, completely strip the bark from the tree and apparently kill it.

Dale Lewis, at the New York Zoological Society, looked at what the tree might get out of this relationship. First he found that the bark rapidly grows back. He also found dozens of seeds intact in the elephants' droppings. The elephants had eaten the fruit and dropped the seeds in well-drained deep soils, away from predators that might eat the seeds (*Biotropica*, vol. 19, p. 50). The seeds greatly benefit from their journey through the elephant's digestive system. They germinate much better than uneaten seeds, and the dung itself helps them to germinate.

The elephant's reputation as a forestry vandal could now be behind it.

Paul Simons, 'The browning of Africa', *New Scientist*, 23 June 1988

There was a furore when it became widely known that several thousand elephants required culling in each of the great elephant-containing national parks and reserves in East, Central and South Africa. Rightly, the public asked: why so many and why so suddenly? The furore gathered momentum when the methods to be used for culling, and use of the products, came into open discussion: should military weapons, poison-filled hypodarts, heavy rifles or bombardment from helicopters be used? . . . The question of the sudden mass slaughter of up to 2,000 elephants in a single operation also required consideration. It seemed proper to them to find some way to utilise the products and to dispose of the carcasses, for there would be too many for disposal by the small populations of scavengers and predators currently extant. Otherwise, it seemed difficult, on the political front, to justify such wastage and massacre. In at least one or two national parks the products of the slaughter were successfully marketed locally. But what of one national park where the drug administered by hypodarts rendered the elephant meat unfit for human consumption, and it had to be either abandoned to scavengers, buried or burned? What of another national park where tenders were invited from foreign meat-packaging firms to can and market the meat as pet food for pampered dogs in Europe and America?

Sylvia K. Sikes, *The Natural History of the African Elephant*, London: Weidenfeld & Nicolson, 1971

His [Ian Parker's] method of killing came of long experience of elephant reactions to gunfire. The tame herds of the Park were an easy prey. Cautiously approaching a group, he and his hunters would let the elephants become aware of something unusual by deliberately breaking twigs, making metallic clicks, or coughing gently; hearing this the elephants, sensing an alien, unidentified presence, would invariably move in towards one another forming a defensive circle with mother facing outwards and the young and the babies tucked between their legs or stowed safely behind a mass of body. The hunters would then close in until they were spread in a semi-circle around the tightly bunched elephants and open fire with semi-automatic rifles of the type used by NATO. The largest cows would be shot first, whereupon the younger members of the group would mill about in hopeless confusion, bereft of leadership but unwilling to abandon their dead leaders. The hunters would swiftly finish off the rest. A group of ten animals usually took no more than 30 seconds to kill. No survivors were ever left and consequently the bad news never spread from one group to the next. The only ones sometimes to be spared were calves between the ages of three and seven; old enough to live without milk from their mothers but young enough to be caught and sold to zoos . . . Little of the carcass was wasted. Meat was sold for local consumption around the Park, the feet were made into umbrella stands, and the entire skin and the ears tanned to make an unusually hard-wearing leather. The ivory was the most valuable commodity of all, and found a ready market.

Ian Parker paid the Park five pounds an elephant.

Ian & Oria Douglas-Hamilton, *Among the Elephants*, London: Collins & Harvill Press, 1975

The violent scramble for ivory seems one of history's inexplicables. Gems are pretty, portable, and rare; gold does not tarnish and is heavy; but ivory cracks, warps, changes colour, is eaten by rats, and breaks easily. Yet it has intrigued men throughout the ages. People who did not know what it was put a high value upon it, and even now, long after the discovery of dozens of other substances that do everything it does, people still pay a high price for it.

This regard for ivory may be partly mystical and have originated in early Stone Age times, when it seems to have acquired a religious connotation bestowed upon objects (notably sculptures in the round) made from this substance which seemed to have qualities of half-life. Ivory, be it Elephant, Hippopotamus, Walrus, Sperm Whale, or even Narwhal or Wild Hog tooth, was derived from the biggest and most impressive local animals. Being the material of which teeth are made, it seemed alive; early man suffered from toothache just as we do and he knew only too well that teeth grow and die. Teeth are the least destructible parts of an animal and they are an animal's ultimate weapon. When a wondrously powerful animal died, you might wear its teeth around your neck not only because they were pretty and durable but because, not being yet wholly dead, they might retain some of the strength and power of the animal.

Ivan T. Sanderson, *The Dynasty of Abu: A History and Natural History of the Elephants and Their Relatives Past and Present*, London: Cassell, 1960

Thrones of ivory stretch across the ages, for there is the ivory throne of Solomon, the ivory throne sent by Hezekiah, King of Judah, as tribute to Sennacherib, the throne of ivory sent to the Etruscan King, Porsenna, and the ivory throne sent from Travancore by its Indian Prince to his Empress, Victoria of Britain. Perhaps we should include the ivory chair, inlaid with gold, of Suleiman the Magnificent, in which he sat while, on the feast of Bairam, all the harem women came to kiss the unspeakable Turkish foot.

E. D. Moore, *Ivory: Scourge of Africa*, London & New York: Harper & Brothers, 1931

Most of sub-Saharan Africa remained inaccessible to the world ivory trade until the 18th and 19th centuries. The main problem was a lack of transport; the solution came in three stages, each accompanied by a more efficient exploitation of elephant populations. The first solution was transport by slaves. As European, American and Arab slave traders opened up routes into the interior of Africa, first from the west and then from the east, more and more elephant populations came under attack.

Petition to Upgrade the African Elephant from Threatened to Endangered Status, Washington, D.C.: The International Wildlife Coalition, December 1988

The slave trade and the ivory trade grew up hand in hand in Africa, and it is therefore almost impossible to disassociate the shooting of elephants from the evils of commercial slavery.

Sylvia K. Sikes, *The Natural History of the African Elephant*, London: Weidenfeld & Nicolson, 1971

With the Roman Empire the demand for ivory exceeded all bounds . . . Roman greed led to a shortage of African ivory in Pliny's day (VIII, 7), though the Indian supply was maintained. The fact that a merchant named Dioscorus adventured as far south as Cape Delgado may suggest the need to probe further afield . . . the demands of the Circus as well as for ivory led to the gradual decrease of elephants in North Africa in the fourth century and their virtual disappearance by the seventh . . .

Tusks were often dedicated in temples and carried in triumphal processions, while the resemblance of ivory to human flesh made it a suitable substance for exposed parts of statues of gods and men. Legend recorded that the gods gave Pelops of Phrygia an artificial ivory shoulder; the ivory statue by the Phrygian king of Cyprus, Pygmalion, even came to life; and Penelope in the Odyssey recalled that lying dreams issued forth from a gate of ivory. In early Italy worked ivory is found in the rich tombs of Etruria and Praeneste and was the privilege of the ruling class. Under Etruscan influence the kings, and later the magistrates of early Rome, adopted it for their insignia of office, their sceptres and curule chairs [chairs for those of the highest rank]. Apart from that, it would be little used in the frugal days of the early Republic, but when eastern luxuries began to flood into Rome from the second century, ivory was among them, and Cicero can speak of 'houses of marble that glitter with ivory and gold' (*marmoreis tectis ebore et auro fulgentibus*). The blatant extravagance of the Empire increased the demand. Caligula gave his horse an ivory stable, while Seneca possessed 500 tripod-tables with ivory legs. 'In literature alone,' wrote E. H. Warmington [Warmington, *The Commerce between the Roman Empire and India*, 1928], 'we find it used for statues, chairs, beds, sceptres, hilts, scabbards, chariots, carriages, tablets, book-covers, table-legs, doors, flutes, lyres, combs, brooches, pins, scrapers, boxes, bird-cages, floors and so on.' Finally, it made its appearance in the splendid diptychs of the early Byzantine period and in the ritual of the Christian church. To pander to these demands of luxury, not to mention of Circus and war, serious inroads were made upon the elephant population of the ancient world, resulting in the total disappearance of two groups, the Syrian and North African.

H. H. Scullard, *The Elephant in the Greek and Roman World*, London: Thames & Hudson, 1974

Nothing creates a greater surprise among the Negroes on the sea-coast, than the eagerness displayed by the European traders to procure elephants' teeth – it being exceedingly difficult to make them comprehend to what use it is applied. Although they are shown knives with ivory hafts, combs, and toys of the same material, and are convinced that the ivory thus manufactured was originally parts of a tooth, they are not satisfied. They suspect that this commodity is more frequently converted in Europe to purposes of far greater importance, the true nature of which is studiously concealed from them, lest the price of ivory should be enhanced. They cannot, they say, easily persuade themselves, that ships would be built, and voyages undertaken, to procure an article which had no other value than that of furnishing handles to knives, &c., when pieces of wood would answer the purpose equally well.

Mungo Park, *Travels in the Interior of Africa*, Edinburgh: Oliver & Boyd, 1816

Every pound weight [of ivory] has cost the life of a man, woman or child; for every five pounds a hut has been burned; for every two tusks a village has been destroyed; every twenty tusks have been obtained at the price of a district with all its people, villages, and plantations.

H. M. Stanley, *How I Found Livingstone: Travels, Adventures, and Discoveries in Central Africa*, London, 1872

When the skull is clean on one side the neck should be cut. This alone is a herculean task. The vertebra severed, the head is turned over by eight or ten men, and the other side similarly cleaned. When both sockets are ready an axe is used to chop them away chip by chip until the tusk is free. This chopping should always be done by an expert, as otherwise large chips off the tusk itself are liable to be taken by the axe.

On this particular occasion no one was at all adept at chopping out, and it was hours before the tusks were freed. Later on my Wanzamwezi boys became very expert indeed at this job, and twelve of them, whose particular job it became, could handle as many as ten bull elephants in a day provided they were not too distant one from the other and that they had plenty of native assistance.

W. D. M. Bell, *The Wanderings of an Elephant Hunter*, Suffolk: Neville Spearman, 1923 (reprinted 1981)

Poachers in India do not shoot indiscriminately into a herd; they carefully select and track a tusker to shoot him. If he is only wounded – and some poachers still use old muzzle-loaders – they will follow the spoor until he collapses, and then hack out the ivory . . .

As a result of this selective poaching, it is not . . . the species as a whole that is threatened, it is the continued presence of tuskers. Tusk development is a genetically determined trait, and in areas of serious poaching, there is clearly a strong selective pressure against the genes which produce tusks. Naresh [Bedi, naturalist and film-maker] told me "Many people are worried that the next generation of elephants will be all *mucknas* [tuskless] because no tuskers are surviving to breed now."

Ian Redmond, 'The Secret Life of the Other Elephant', *BBC Wildlife*, 5: 12, December 1987

Served the inevitable tea, we listen to the manager explain his ivorycutting works. He is flanked by very large ivory carvings of the most intricate design and workmanship. Whenever he tells about his quotas being exceeded, we clap, and he claps as well.

'How much ivory do you use a year?'

'Several hundred tons.'

'Isn't the elephant an endangered species?'

The question is ignored, but as we progress through the factory, we are told the employees believe elephants drop their tusks once a year. One of our group, dividing the weight of an average tusk into 200 tons, figures it would take 400 elephants to keep this plant supplied with ivory for a full 12 months.

It's hot in the factory and almost every craftsman works under the wash of electric fans. Much of the intricate detail in the tusks is created by electric hand-drills or drills so tiny they resemble dental equipment. All the shavings and ivory dust are saved to form composition material.

Richard Lloyd Jones, Jr, 'China: from Carving to Caves', Oklahoma: *Tulsa Tribune*, 27 November 1978

It [ivory] has continued to rise to its present level of about $150 per kilo, and as such represents an irresistible temptation to organised crime . . . to the criminal mind, a herd of elephants has become analogous to a bank vault, to be cracked with whatever fire-power is considered necessary. The fact that ivory poachers are prepared to kill park rangers is indicative of the scale of the problem.

Petition to Upgrade the African Elephant from Threatened to Endangered Status, Washington, D.C.: The International Wildlife Coalition, December 1988

In 1979 one of us (I.P.) completed a survey of the world ivory trade for Dr Iain Douglas-Hamilton on behalf of IUCN [International Union for Conservation of Nature and Natural Resources] and the US Fish and Wildlife Service. This indicated that total exports of raw ivory from Africa had been of the order of 680,000 kg in 1980 [37,482 elephants]. There will, of course, be an additional element of illegal ivory smuggled, but this is likely to be small, for by far the most widespread method of getting illegal tusks out of Africa has been to 'legalize' them. By bribery and other devices, legal documents have been obtained to cover their export, so that the tusks arrive at their overseas destinations quite openly and indistinguishable from ivory of legitimate origin.

I. S. C. Parker & Esmond Bradley Martin, 'How Many Elephants are Killed for the Ivory Trade?' *Oryx*, 3: 15, 235–9, 1982

The United States, as one of the world's major consumers of ivory, has a clear responsibility to set a high standard for elephant conservation . . . There is also evidence that lack of enforcement of existing laws in the US, such as the Lacey Act, has enabled large quantities of illegal ivory to enter the USA . . .

The total value of the US imports of elephant products (skins as well as ivory) in the years 1984–86 averaged $29 million per annum. TRAFFIC estimated that the total retail value was in excess of $100 million . . . the number of elephants killed for the US market during 1983–86 is a minimum of 12,934 . . . In 1986, the number of elephants killed to supply the US market for worked ivory amounts to 32,254. And 75 per cent of that year's imports were declared as originating in African countries which had prohibited ivory exports – making them illegal imports under the Lacey Act. Other violations of the Lacey Act include the import of 903 tusks and 1,680 kg of raw ivory during 1983–84 from Zaire, when that country had banned the export of ivory in 1978 . . . worse still, in terms of conservation, was a shipment of 425 tusks from India, where the endangered Asian elephant, *Elephas maximus*, occurs.

Petition to Upgrade the African Elephant from Threatened to Endangered Status, Washington, D.C.: The International Wildlife Coalition, December 1988

The greatest single use for ivory in Japan today is for making seals. It surprises many westerners that the Japanese do not use personal signatures to endorse bank cheques, contracts or documents. Instead every adult has his or her personal seal [*hanko*]. The design is unique to each individual, and, as one's seal has to last a lifetime, it is made out of durable materials ranging from wood to crystal, precious metals and ivory. Ivory seals are by far the most popular and sought after. There are a variety of reasons for this. Perhaps the most important is that there is a traditional connection between ivory and wealth. Ivory is a status symbol – as it has always been. It also has functional qualities. It is very slightly absorbent, which makes it better than metals for transferring ink from pad to paper. Only African hard ivory is used for seals and lasts a lifetime without perceptible wear. It also has an attractive 'feel' about it.

Mohamed Amin & Ian Parker, *Ivory Crisis*, London: Chatto & Windus, 1983

Here and there it [ivory] persists in some specialist role. It forms the joints in bagpipes. It provides the veneers for piano keys. Once most pianos had ivory keys, today only the very best have them. Virtuosos insist on ivory keys, apparently for the feel. On paper such reasons seem trite, and I thought it was affectation – until I felt the difference for myself. However, the amount of ivory required for piano keys is very small. Only large tusks of more than 40 lbs are used, and these come in the main from male elephants past their prime.

Mohamed Amin & Ian Parker, *Ivory Crisis*, London: Chatto & Windus, 1983

The most bizarre use of ivory that I have come across is the painting of pornographic scenes on ivory plaques. India is the main producer of such work, although the plaques are also made in Hong Kong, while Spain is the major market.

Mohamed Amin & Ian Parker, *Ivory Crisis*, London: Chatto & Windus, 1983

The last thing that the Japanese ivory merchants want is the disappearance of the African elephant . . .

Mohamed Amin & Ian Parker, *Ivory Crisis*, London: Chatto & Windus, 1983

Ivory can be used to purchase weapons; there are, for example, reports that UNITA has slaughtered perhaps 100,000 elephants to pay South Africa for its support in the war in Angola.

Petition to Upgrade the African Elephant from Threatened to Endangered Status, Washington, D.C.: The International Wildlife Coalition, December 1988

In Uganda's national parks, dead elephants outnumber the living. Their rotting carcasses litter this tragic and beautiful country. For every elephant left alive, there are now two rotting hulks of skin and bones, the flesh untouched except by vultures, but the tusks hacked out by ivory poachers who have brought the great herds to the edge of extinction . . . eight years of misrule by Idi Amin and the descent into chaos after his downfall have all but finished the game reserves which were once the pride of East Africa. Uganda's recent history of conflict and confusion has hitherto prevented wildlife experts from obtaining a true picture of the situation. Now, for the first time, a survey conducted by Dr. Robert Malpas, a British zoologist, reveals the full extent of the slaughter in the parks . . .

The contents make grim reading. Ten years ago there were more than 2,000 elephants in Rwenzori national park alone. Today, fewer than that number remain in the whole of Uganda. In Rwenzori barely 150 survive – all but a handful huddled with touching trust around the tourist lodge at Mweya.

On their first day in Rwenzori, the survey team heard gunshots and later found five dead elephants swarming with vultures. No meat had been cut but the tusks had gone. The animals had been killed solely for ivory.

Most of the carcasses were found in groups – clear evidence that modern semi-automatic weapons have replaced the poachers' traditional armoury of poisoned arrows, snares and bananas laced with battery acid.

In one group, five female elephants were found within a few yards of each other, as if they had huddled together for protection. Inside one skeleton lay the bones of an unborn calf.

'Unless current trends are immediately arrested,' warns the report, 'the Rwenzori elephants will be eradicated in a matter of months rather than years.'

Brian Jackman, 'Requiem for the Pride of Africa', *Sunday Times*, 7 December 1980

A survey of stocks of elephants in Africa makes grim reading of how they are being sacrificed for their tusks. A report in *Oryx* by Douglas-Hamilton, a wildlife conservation expert, describes what could be 'one of the most wasteful mammalian tragedies of this century' . . . Today elephant numbers are declining (contrary to previous reports) much more rapidly throughout that continent – especially since 1970.

According to Mr Douglas-Hamilton, the two most important factors are the proliferation of automatic weapons and other heavy guns, and the huge rise in the price of ivory from $5.45 a kilo in 1969 to over $100.00 a kilo . . .

Political chaos in the past 15 years has multiplied the numbers of soldiers and insurgents. Powerful weaponry, especially automatic rifles, has found its way into the hands of poachers and poorly disciplined irregulars.

Game wardens are often powerless to help them. In one instance, in Mozambique, pitched battles were fought between rebels and wildlife department staff.

Examples of the slaughter of wildlife are horrific. Elephant numbers in the Central African Republic and Uganda have declined by 80 per cent since the late 1970s. Out of 15,000 elephants in Chad before 1979, only 2,000 to 3,000 remain after the outbreak of civil war.

Poachers armed with Kalashnikov rifles, often mounted on horse or camel, are responsible for the collapse of many elephant herds in the Sudan. An anti-poaching unit found groups of up to 80 dead elephants in western Somali. In parts of Zaire elephants, once abundant, are no longer to be seen, and those in the north are under constant threat from Sudanese poachers. Even in Tanzania and Kenya significant reduction of numbers has occurred since 1970.

The ultimate object is ivory, much of which is exported to the Far East. A reflection of this sickening situation is the reduction of mean tusk weights obtained from Hong Kong and Japanese ivory imports (from 16.3 kilos in 1979 to 9.7 kilos in 1982 for Japan) and the very low mean tusk weights of ivory confiscated from poachers in Uganda and the Central African Republic. Smaller and younger elephants are now being killed for ivory under conditions of severe over-exploitation.

If measures are not implemented soon, the outlook for elephants in Africa is bleak.

Simon Davis, 'Ivory poachers could wipe out elephants', Science report, *The Times*, 2 April 1987

Ivory hunters are still slaughtering elephants by the thousand and some experts are warning that if the killing isn't stopped the African elephant could be almost extinct within 10 years. The lure for the poachers is the price of ivory. In 1971 an 11 lb. tusk was worth $11. Now it will make $1000 – as much as some game wardens earn in a year. The worst slaughter has been in the Central African Republic, Zaire, Congo, Gabon, Sudan, Uganda, Tanzania, Gambia and Kenya. The region's elephant population has fallen 80% in the last decade. In 2 years 1,400 tonnes of ivory have been exported from Central Africa, which means more than 150,000 elephants have been killed. Just a decade ago there were 120,000 elephants in Kenya. A journey through the Tsavo National Park today reveals the slaughter that threatens to wipe out the great beast. The manner of their killing is particularly brutal. Chainsaws were used to cut the tusks from their faces. Since the seventies it is estimated that 85% of Kenya's elephant population has died in this way. Daphne Sheldrick runs an orphanage for baby elephants whose mothers have been killed by poachers . . . Daphne Sheldrick accepts she's fighting a losing battle: 'Something must be done to stop the demand for ivory, to stop people in America, Britain and places like that buying the end result, the carved ivory. After all, no-one needs ivory, but, as long as there's a demand for ivory, elephants are going to be killed in Africa.'

ITN Bulletin, *News At Ten*, broadcast 3 December 1988

If the annual ivory harvest continues, it will eliminate the elephants in eight to 10 years.

Todd Shields, Nairobi, 'Elephants massacred for ivory', London: *Independent*, 4 April 1988

It may well be that if the elephant never had become part of man's religious ritual, none would be alive today.

Don Livingstone, quoted in David Gucwa & James Ehmann *To Whom It May Concern: An Investigation of the Art of Elephants*, New York: W. W. Norton, 1985

In Pali scriptures it is duly set forth 'that the form under which Buddha will descend to the earth for the last time, will be that of a beautiful young white elephant, open-jawed, with a head the colour of cochineal, with tusks shining like silver sparkling with gems, covered with a splendid netting of gold, perfect in its organs and limbs, and majestic in appearance.'

Charles Frederick Holder, *The Ivory King*, New York: Scribner, 1888

The sanctity of a white elephant dates from the earliest period of Buddhist history. Indra himself rode on a *three*-headed elephant. When Gaudama entered the womb of the queen to be born on earth for the last time, it was in the form of an elephant . . . a 'white' elephant, however few the pale spots he may have, is revered throughout the breadth and length of the land. One of the King of Siam's proudest titles, as is well known, is 'Lord of the White Elephant'.

Carl Bock, *Temples and Elephants: Travels in Siam in 1881–1882*, London: Sampson Low, Marston, Searle, & Rivington, 1884

With the white elephant some vague notions of a vital Buddha are associated, and there can be no doubt that the marvellous sagacity of the creatures has served to strengthen their [the Singhalese] religious prejudices. Siamese have been known to whisper their secrets into an elephant's ear, and to ask a solution of their perplexities by some sign or movement. And most assuredly there is more sense and reason in the worship of an intelligent beast than in that of sticks and stones, the work of men's hands.

Charles Frederick Holder, *The Ivory King: A Popular History of the Elephant and its Allies*, New York: Scribner 1886

Then came the great elephant . . . the wise elephant, that is our Lord Jesus Christ. Greater than all, he is made the smallest of all. Being wounded he bore our infirmities and carried our sins.

Bestiary, Harleian Manuscript 3244, British Museum (probably deriving from the *Liber Physiologus*, compiled by a Greek monk of Alexandria)

Better to live alone; with a fool there is no companionship. With few desires, live alone and do no evil, like an elephant in the forest, roaming at will.

Suttapitaka, *Dhammapada*

And, above all others, we should protect and hold sacred those types, Nature's masterpieces, which are first singled out for destruction on account of their size, or splendour, or rarity, and that false detestable glory which is accorded to their most detestable slayers. In ancient times the spirit of life shone brightest in these; and when others that shared the earth with them were taken by death they were left, being more worthy of perpetuation. Like

immortal flowers they have drifted down to us on the ocean of time, and their strangeness and beauty bring to our imaginations a dream and a picture of that unknown world, immeasurably far removed, where man was not: and when they perish, something of gladness goes out from nature, and the sunshine loses something of its brightness.

W. H. Hudson, *The Naturalist in La Plata*, London: Chapman & Hall, 1892

Its breath is said to be a cure for headaches in man.
Cassiodorus, *Variae*, X, 30

Elephants are very special animals: intelligent, complicated, intense, ten-der, powerful, and funny. I consider myself immensely fortunate to have spent so much time with them. I have followed the lives of Amboseli's elephants through droughts to periods of superabundance, through times of heavy poaching and great losses to times of peace and relative security. I have watched them give birth and I have watched them die. I have observed young females reach sexual maturity and mate for the first time and young males leave the security of their families and strike out on their own. I have seen the grand old matriarchs leading and defending their families and I have also seen them lose all dignity and run around in play with their tails curled up over their backs and a wild glint in their eyes. I have always said that watching elephants is like reading an engrossing, convoluted novel that I cannot put down but I also do not want to end.

Cynthia Moss, *Elephant Memories: Thirteen Years in the Life of an Elephant Family*, London: Elm Tree Books, 1988

The elephant is probably one of the very few species of mammal whose use to man as a domesticated animal is drawing to a close. As a symbol of power and for pageantry in the Ancient World and in the Far East the elephant has no peer but there can be little future for these roles in the modern world of machinery. It may be questioned what relevance the hunting of mammoths and the ivory trade has to do with the history of domestication, but the elephant is unlike other domesticated animals in that its exploitation by man has not conformed to the usual pattern of taming, and artificial selection following breeding in captivity. Elephants have never been enfolded within human society like the horse or the pig have been. Nevertheless elephants of all races have been closely involved with humans for perhaps half a million years and it will be mankind's loss if we continue the process of extermination that was begun by Palaeolithic man on the mammoth.

Juliet Clutton-Brock, *A Natural History of Domesticated Mammals*, Cambridge: Cambridge University Press, 1987

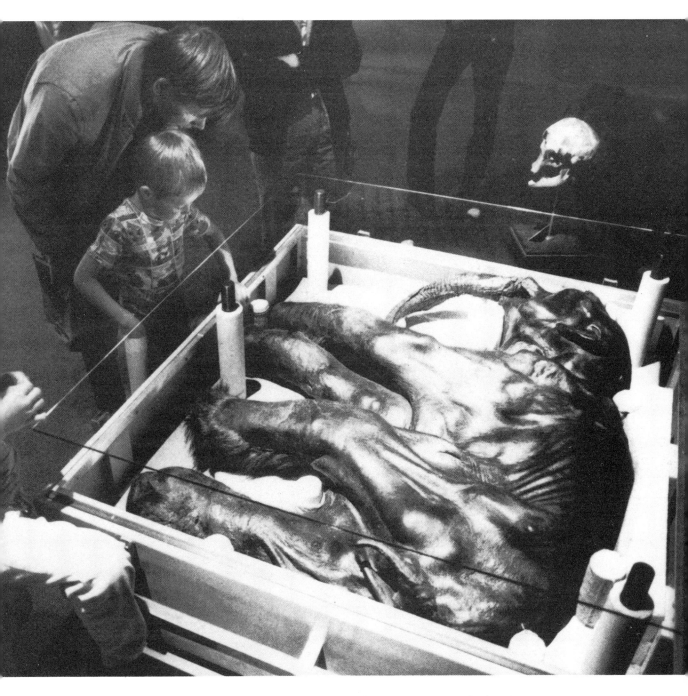

The young show respect for the old. They give place to them in feeding and drinking; they never abandon the weak, even when being hunted; they help the old out of pits when they have fallen in; the females never desert their young. Where, I should like to know, did an elephant ever belabour its sire with blows?

Aelian, *De Natura Animalium*, VI, 61, & VII, 15

Had we known no other animate life-form than our own, we should have been utterly mysterious to ourselves as a species.

Mary Midgley, *Beast & Man: The Roots of Human Nature*, Brighton: Harvester, 1979

What happens to beasts will happen to man. All things are connected. If the great beasts are gone, man would surely die of a great loneliness of spirit.

Chief Seattle of the Nez Perce, 1884

For that which befalleth the sons of men befalleth beasts; even one thing that befalleth them: as the one dieth, so dieth the other; yea, they have all one breath, so that a man hath no pre-eminence above a beast, for all is vanity.

Ecclesiastes 3:19

Acknowledgments
and Index

Acknowledgments

Grateful acknowledgments to Cynthia Moss of the Amboseli Elephant Research Project;
Sue Gooders of Ardea; Joan Ball; Richard Gombrich and Bruce Graham of Balliol College;
Peter Beard; Dr Hans Becker; Tony Bennett; Guy Bentinck; Jordan Bojilov; The Bombay
Natural History Society; Richard Haywood of the British Library; James Bulleitt; Jerome
Byrne, Ned Chaillet; Stephen R. L. Clark; Jill and Richard Courtauld; Clive Curtis; Brian
Doel; Iain Douglas-Hamilton; Randall L. Eaton; James Ehmann; Jeheskel Shoshani of
the Elephant Interest Group, Wayne State University; Peregrine Eliot; Dave Curry and
Allen Thornton of the Environmental Investigation Agency; Lesley Fairbairn; Karl-Erik
Fichtelius; Clive Friend; Richard Goodwin; Ros Reeve of Greenpeace; David Gucwa;
Alec Guinness; Rebecca Hall; Jane Hill; Ethan Hoffman; Andrew Mead of the Hulton
Picture Company; Trevor Ingman; Elisabeth Mann Borgese of the International Ocean
Institute, Valletta; The International Wildlife Coalition; Brian Jackman; Cathy
Arrington, Tim Chester, Tony Colwell, Ian Craig, Annelise Evans, Annabel Fox, Tom
Maschler, Mon Mohan, Gaye Poulton, Polly Samson, Elizabeth Smith and Hilary Turner
of Jonathan Cape; Reinhard Künkel; Louise Landes-Levi; Hilary Lewis; Lillian Lewis;
Kate Wilton of Liskeard Library; Chris Bray, Gilly Hancox, Lawrence Roberts and
Pauline Thompson of Logo Design; Christopher Logue; Asphodel Pauline Long; Oliver
Taplin of Magdalen College; The Mansell Collection; Mao Xianghwa; Professor Eric
Denton of the Marine Biology Research Association; John May; Roger Mayne; Mary
Midgley; Elaine Morgan; Cynthia Moss; Michael Marten; Virginia Kennedy of *Nature*;
Nigel Allen, Clare Boniface, Andrea Caunter, Paul Huxham and Elizabeth Rothwell of
Nexus Colour Laboratories; Guy Nicholls; Patrick and Peggy O'Connor; Brian Servis of
Optikos; Graham Ovenden; Gabi Pape; Ernest, Jean and Deborah Parkins; Liz Nash and
Michael Sewell of the Polytechnic Bookshop, Plymouth; Rex Pyke; Ian Redmond; Kevin
Reilly; Russ Aisthorpe of RMA Recording; George Rodger; Ann Ronan; Esther Samson;
Amanda Sebestyen; Diana Senior; Bill Dow and Tippi Hedren of the Shambala
Foundation; Paul Shepard; Paul Sieveking; Sylvia K. Sikes; John S. Starr; Sue Harrison
of Survival Anglia; Anne R. McGrath of the Thoreau Lyceum; Pat Redfern of Topham;
Simon Trevor; John Warner; Elizabeth Williams; Susan Williams; Joe Winnington;
Michael J. Woods; Elisabeth Woodthorpe; Caroline Younger; William Travers of Zoo
Check; Heidrun Böhm and Lutz Kroth of Zweitausendeins – *imo pectore*.

The publishers and I would also like to thank the following for their kind permission to
reproduce illustrations: Aberham, IFA-Bilderteam (p.33 bottom); Mohamed Amin,
Camerapix (pp. 38, 168); K. and K. Ammann, Ace Photo Agency (p. 22); Karl Ammann,
Ace Photo Agency (p. 28) and Bruce Coleman Inc. (p. 32 top); Heather Angel (p. 60 top);
Archiv für Kunst und Geschichte, Berlin (pp. 154, 162); Art Directors (cover and p. 45);
Jen and Des Bartlett, Survival Anglia (p. 13); Peter Beard (pp. 164-5) and from his
collection (p. 147 top and bottom); John Blake (p. 54 top); Fredrik D. Bodin, Stock,
Boston (p. 118); K. Boldt, Biofoto (pp. 138, 139); Adrian Boyd, Colorific (p. 33 top);
R. Burrel, Frank Spooner Pictures (p. 67 bottom right); Mike Busselle, Photographers'
Library (p. 69 bottom); Butlins Ltd (p. 83 right); Robert Caputo, Stock, Boston (p. 73);
Piers Cavendish, Reflex (pp. 27 top, 48 top, 49 bottom right); David Cayless, Oxford
Scientific Films (p. 25 bottom); Christine Osborne Pictures/MEPP (p. 49 top); Ginette
Cros, Explorer (p. 11 bottom right); Gerald Cubitt (p. 48 bottom); Bruce Davidson,
Survival Anglia (pp. 27 bottom, 61 bottom); A. Deschryver, Tierbilder Okapia (pp. 20
bottom, 29 bottom, 30 top); Deutsche Presse Agentur Gmbh (p. 61 top); Bill Dow (pp. 42
top left, 126 left and right); Jill Freedman, Archive Pictures (pp. 12, 56, 57 middle left, 58

top, 123, 134, 143); Clive Friend, 'Medallion from 3rd century B.C., depicting Queen Mahamaya's dream, from the Bharhut Stupa, Nagpur' (p. 11 bottom left); Ingo Gerlach, Tierbilder Okapia (p. 40); N. Gibbons (p. 66); Brian Gibbs, Barnaby's Picture Library (p. 83 left); Nick Greaves, Planet Earth Pictures (pp. 78-9); Joanna van Gruisan, Ardea London Ltd (p. 67 bottom left); Dr Bernhard Grzimek, Tierbilder Okapia (p. 156 bottom left); David Gucwa (pp. 100 left and right, 166, 176); Clem Haagner, Ardea London Ltd (pp. 17 top, 24 top); P. C. Howard, Aquila Photographics Ltd (p. 75 bottom); Hulton Picture Company (pp. 57 bottom left, 59, 102, 142, 146, 156 top left and right, 161, 163); IFA-Bilderteam (p. 31); Masahiro Iijima, Ardea London Ltd (pp. 18 top, 39); Bo Jarner, Pressehuset (p. 113); John Topham Picture Agency (pp. 50 bottom, 81, 149, 167); D. Kerwin, Ace Photo Agency (p. 21); Gerard Kremer, Explorer (p. 11 top); Reinhard Künkel (pp. 20 top, 65, 69 middle, 87, 110); Charles Lenars, Explorer (p. 8 bottom); Dr W. Lenthold, Tierbilder Okapia (p. 121); George W. 'Slim' Lewis (pp. 42 top right, 64); K. R. Lewis, Northern Picture Library (p. 8 top); McDougall, Tierbilder Okapia (p. 156 bottom right); Martin Library (p. 9 bottom); Ben Martin, Colorific (p. 2); O. Mayer, Action Press (p. 37); Mike Mazzaschi, Stock, Boston (p. 57 middle right); Dilip Mehta, Contact Press Images (p. 49 bottom left); Ulli Michel, Popperfoto (p. 108); Robert Mitchell (p. 16 bottom); Mike Mockler, Swift Picture Library (p. 23 bottom); D. Morris, Ardea London Ltd (p. 69 top); Graham Ovenden (p. 75 top); Oxford Scientific Films (p. 129 top); Paul Popper Ltd (p. 57 bottom right); Klaus Paysan (pp. 14-15, 16 top, 17 bottom, 18 bottom, 32 bottom, 42 bottom); Photo Adelheid Heine Stillmark (p. 68); Photo Library International (p. 71 top); Photri Inc. (pp. 57 top right, 58 bottom); Dieter and Mary Plage, Bruce Coleman UK Ltd (pp. 50 top, 68 bottom, 70); K. G. Preston-Mafham, Premaphotos (p. 43 top and bottom); M. S. Price, Natural Science Photos (p. 30 bottom); private collections (pp. 51, 52 all, 53 all); R. N. Quigley, Photo Library International (p. 54 bottom); Mandel Ranjit, Frank Lane Picture Agency (p. 111); E. Hanumantha Rao, NHPA (p. 7 bottom); Mike Read, Swift Picture Library (p. 10 top); Ian Redmond (pp. 23 top, 71 bottom, 91, 130, 157); George Rodger (p. 170); Alan Root, Tierbilder Okapia (pp. 29 top, 153); George Roshan, Northern Picture Library (p. 72); E. S. Ross (p. 76); Leonard Lee Rue III, Stock, Boston (p. 89); Michael St Maur Sheil, Susan Griggs Agency (p. 26); Peter Sanders (pp. 44-5); Jonathan Scott, Planet Earth Pictures (pp. 24 bottom right, 33 middle); Shirt Off Your Back Picture Agency (pp. 1, 4-5, 34-5, 47, 55, 57 top left, 62, 63 all); John Stewart (p. 129 bottom); Tierbilder Okapia (pp. 25 top, 136 bottom left); Tony Stone Worldwide (p. 67 top); Simon Trevor, from his film 'Bloody Ivory', (pp. 19 all, 36 all, 74 top four, 77 all); P. H. & S. L. Ward, Natural Science Photographs (p. 7 top); Ben Weaver, American Broadcasting Company (p. 24 bottom left); Rodney Wood, Planet Earth Pictures (p. 86); G. Ziesler, Bruce Coleman UK Ltd (p. 74 bottom).

The publishers and I have made strenuous efforts to obtain necessary permissions with reference to copyright material, both illustrative and quoted, but there are some owners we have been unable to trace. If they would write to us, we shall be pleased to acknowledge them in any future edition.

Index

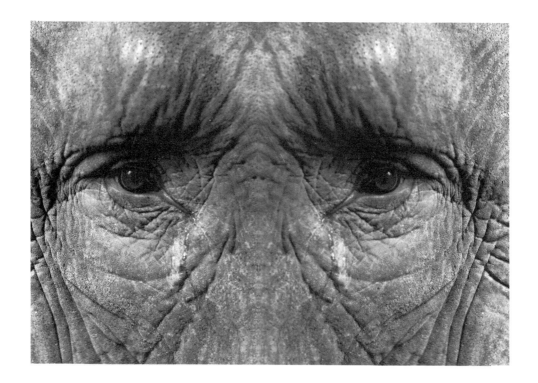

Copyright © 1989 by Heathcote Williams

Published by Harmony Books, a division of Crown Publishers, Inc.,
201 East 50th Street, New York, New York 10022
Originally published in Great Britain by Jonathan Cape Ltd

HARMONY and colophon are trademarks of Crown Publishers, Inc.

Manufactured in Italy

Library of Congress Cataloging-in-Publication Data
Williams. Heathcote
Sacred elephant/by Heathcote Williams.
176 pp. 29 × 19.4cm.
Summary: The author's poem raises our consciousness that a gentle
sensitive animal is being forced into labor and slaughtered for jewelry.

1. Elephants – Poetry.   [1. Elephants – Poetry. 2. English poetry.]
I. Title
PR6073.I4278S23   1989
821'.914 – dc20
89-11149
CIP
AC
ISBN 0-517-57547-7
ISBN 0-517-57320-2 (pbk.)

10 9 8 7 6 5 4 3 2 1

First American Edition